By the Same Author

BIOGRAPHICAL WORKS

Bloomsbury, A House of Lions
The Life of Henry James
James Joyce: The Last Journey
Henry David Thoreau
Willa Cather (with E. K. Brown)
The Diary of Alice James
Literary Biography

CRITICAL WORKS

The Modern Psychological Novel
Stuff of Sleep and Dreams

EDITOR OF

Henry James

Letters (four volumes)
The Complete Plays
The Complete Tales (twelve volumes)
The Bodley Head James
Tales of the Supernatural

Edmund Wilson

The Twenties: from Notebooks & Diaries of the Period
The Thirties
The Forties

Writing Lives

Principia Biographica

LEON EDEL

Writing Lives

Principia Biographica

Yes—writing lives is the devil!

Virginia Woolf

W. W. NORTON & COMPANY

NEW YORK / LONDON

The following excerpts are reprinted from *The New York Times*: "The Final Chord
of the Quintet," by Leon Edel, February 6, 1972, Book Review; "A Biographer's
Trip to the Past is Déjà Vu with a Difference," by Leon Edel, January 21, 1973,
Travel Section. Copyright © 1972/73 by The New York Times Company. Reprinted
by permission.

The text of this book is composed in Granjon, with display type set in Garamond.
Composition and manufacturing by The Maple-Vail Book Manufacturing Group
Book design by Guy Fleming

First Edition

Library of Congress Cataloging in Publication Data

Edel, Leon, 1907–
    Writing lives.

    Bibliography: p.
    Includes index.
    1. Biography (as a literary form)   I. Title.
CT21.E33   1985   808'.06692   84-5959

ISBN 0-393-01882-2

W. W. Norton & Company, Inc., 500 Fifth Avenue, New York, N.Y. 10110
W. W. Norton & Company Ltd., 37 Great Russell Street, London WC1B 3NU

1 2 3 4 5 6 7 8 9 0

To Rupert Hart-Davis

HOMAGE AND AFFECTION

CONTENTS

CONTENTS

PART TWO

Writing Lives

Principia Biographica

Introduction

IN THE FORM OF

A MANIFESTO

Biographers write lives.

Some write biographies because they have fallen in love with their subjects (as Boswell fell in love with Johnson.) Some make biography into their trade: they seek lively and lucrative subjects, celebrities and popular lives—actresses, murderers, tycoons, gangsters, presidents. All biographers understandably seek a measure of fame for themselves. A few—a very few—write biographies because they like the energy and economy, the order and form of a work of art.

A writer of lives is allowed the imagination of form but not of fact.

Biography attempts to preserve what it can of human greatness or humbleness; to describe a pilgrimage from childhood to maturity and finally to the grave, and in this process the labors, errors, passions and actions that lead to accomplishment. Few "ordinary" lives are written. One supposes that readers do not want to read about the ordinary but the extraordinary.

The writing of lives is a department of history and is closely related to the discoveries of history. It can claim the same skills. No lives are led outside history or society; they take place in human time. No biography is complete unless it reveals the individual within history, within an ethos and a social complex. In saying this we remember Donne: no man is an island unto himself.

The relation of the biographer to the subject is the very core of the biographical enterprise. Idealization of the hero or the heroine blinds the writer of lives to the meaning of the materials. Hatred or animosity does the same. But most biographies tend to be written in affection and love. If there ensues an emotional involvement on the part of the biographer he or she must be reminded that love is blind. Psychology calls this "transference."

We must recognize that not all biographers can be artists. A properly assembled documentary biography is in effect a kind of miniarchive. It may possess the organizing imagination but cannot lay claim to art. As for the shovelled-together work, it remains a clutter.

In a sense all lives are clutter composed as the poet said of "the butt-ends of my days and ways." If biography reproduces this it reproduces habitual disorder. Robert Louis Stevenson once wrote: "Life is monstrous, infinite, illogical, abrupt and poignant; a work of art, in comparison, is neat, finite, self-contained, rational, flowing, emasculate. Life imposes by brute energy, like inarticulate thunder; art catches the ear among the far louder noises of experience like an air artificially made by a discreet musician." If we apply these words to biography we can see that a writer of lives must extract individuals from their chaos yet create an illusion that they are in the midst of life—in the way that a painter arrives at an approximation of a familiar visage on canvas. The biographer who is unable to do this creates a waxworks, a dummy, a papier-mâché, and often a caricature.

The fancy of the biographer—we repeat—resides in the art of narration, not in the substance of the story. The substance exists before the narration begins.

Are biographies a form of fiction? Some critics hold this belief. But they are wrong. In a novel, the novelist knows everything about the hero or heroine. His characters are his own invention and he can do what he wishes with them. Novelists have omniscience. Biographers never do. The personages exist; the documents exist; they are the "givens" to a writer of lives. They may not be altered. To alter is to disfigure. A biographer may meditate on the habits and conditions of the personages; he may study their psychology; but he meditates on preexisting persons, some well known before they reach his printed page.

Also the mind and inner world of the subject is unique and cannot be fashioned by anyone else. The biographer may not substitute his mind or fantasy for that of the subject. Indeed the subject's inwardness can be recreated only in a limited way and only if sufficient self-communion has been bequeathed in diaries, letters, meditations, dreams.

We must never forget that like other literary artists, the biographer works in words. A novelist can create imaginary conversations. But a biographer can only use conversation when such conversation has been recorded in notes and minutes or on tapes. Biographical narratives draw with caution on table-talk. They use life residues—laundry lists, unpaid bills, check stubs, notes, gossip, memories, and in modern times the detritus of the computer.

This suggests that lives are composed in most instances as if they were mosaics. Mosaics, before they are composed, are not fiction; they are an accumulation of little pieces of reality, shaped into an image. The danger of fiction resides in fanciful arrangement of these pieces of reality.

In the biographical process the biographer is, as Desmond MacCarthy said, an artist under oath. To be sure, some artists perjure themselves. It is the task of critics to unmask the perjurors.

Introduction

The poet is the poem; the novelist the novel; the play-wright the play. Is the biographer the biography?

A biographer who works as an artist becomes the biography. An "impersonal" biography is tasteless and without character, force or authority. "The thing that is necessarily overlooked," said Wallace Stevens "is the presence of the determining personality." Why "necessarily?" A good and useful life must be fashioned by a "determining personality." The biographer unable to select and arrange significant detail is like a painter who smudges his canvas.

The biographer truly succeeds if a distinct literary form can be found for the particular life.

Byron once wrote that "one lies more to one's self than to anyone else." The biographer needs to discover human self-deceptions (or defenses, which they usually are). Such deceptions may become a covert life-myth out of which lives—and biographies—are fashioned.

Biography works in mysteries. That is its fascination.

"Yes," said Virginia Woolf "writing lives is the devil!"

PART ONE

The New Biography

·

BIOGRAPHY is a noble and adventurous art, as noble as the making of painted portraits, poems, statues. We know how a painter can give voices to an entire wall; and a sculptor, with skill of chisel and eye, can bring durable life to clay. So a biographer fashions a man or woman out of documents, words. Poetry talks in images and symbols. A novelist, in his omniscience, knows the measure of his characters, out of his passion for all sorts and conditions of human life. The biographer, however, begins with certain limiting little facts. "How" exclaimed Virginia Woolf when she sat down to write the life of her friend Roger Fry—"how can one make a life out of six cardboard boxes full of tailors' bills, love letters and old picture post-cards?" How indeed? Yet Virginia Woolf was able to construct a singular life by using such facts as she possessed and bridging the silences with the poetry of her observing and constructing imagination. Her biographer friend Lytton Strachey spoke of his art as "the most delicate and humane of all the branches of the art of writing." No more delicate, I am sure, than verse, or certain forms of drama. Biography, however, has a particular kind of delicacy. It seeks to evoke life out of inert materials—in a shoebox or an attic—records of endeavor and imagination, cupidity and terror, kindness and love. Strachey called the writing of lives "humane," I believe, because it deals with strange volatile delicately-orchestrated beings, not mythical gods. The ambiguous records are packed with the contradictions of life itself. Perhaps this is what Yeats implied when he wrote "we may come to think that nothing exists but a stream of souls, that all knowledge is biography." Is it not true that all that we know, all that we discover, all that we feel, comes from this stream of souls, and from our own soul or inwardness—human stuff and human sagacity. Every step forward or backward in civilization has been a human step.

Not all artists or historians have such an exalted notion of biography. Some feel it to be a prying, peeping and even predatory process. Biography has been called "a disease of English literature" (George Eliot); professional biographers have been called "hyenas" (Edward Sackville-West). They have also been called "psycho-plagiarists" (Nabokov) and biography has been said to be "always superfluous" and "usually in bad taste" (Auden). Nabokov and Auden felt strongly that lives of individuals who were writers cannot and should not be written. The works writers create—the traced imaginations—suffice; they would argue no personal gloss is required. The "new criticism" certainly held to this view: the "biographical fallacy" was critical dogma. It is the work not the life, they said, that counts. In using the word "psycho-plagiarist" Nabokov suggests that biographers are individuals who somehow complete their own lives by writing the lives of others. Such identifications might indeed be called a form of plagiarism; the biographer totally immerses his Self in the Self of his subject. According to Nabokov, he seeks to fortify or reconstruct his own ego by using someone else's. Proust said as much of critics: they were incomplete men, he said, who complete themselves with the work of another. Nevertheless, in biography, whatever the biographer's motivations, a work takes its form, for better or worse. And if the work counts, it is like the breath of the human body, and that body counts as well. A writer writes out of his whole physical as well as mental being. I am not sure the work and the life can be dissociated.

Written lives engender strong feelings. Yet the biographer works within the unavoidable limitations and restraints of which Virginia Woolf spoke. Biography, we must remind ourselves, is a nascent art even though hundreds of lives are written every year. And it is a vulnerable art. The anti-biography of Nabokov and Auden reflects artistic reticences. Auden's repeated assertion that biography is "superfluous" may indeed have been more than fear of revelations or even a belief in the sufficiency of his own works. He kept few secrets from his readers. There wasn't much to reveal: his homosexuality was known. Perhaps he felt no further dredging was required. Certainly he had read a great many incompetent biographies. Perhaps he was frightened—enough bad lives are published to frighten any great man. And Auden, moreover, was not alone. William Makepeace Thackeray died commanding that there be "no biography." Matthew Arnold did the same. And, in our time, T. S. Eliot. But Eliot also said that "the line between curiosity which is legitimate and that which is merely harmless, and between that which is merely harmless and that which is vulgarly impertinent, can never be precisely drawn." Henry James went much further. He called down Shakespeare's curse on any one who might try to stir his bones. Let us add that Arnold and Thackeray almost succeeded. Their heirs obediently lowered a curtain. They shut all the doors. When the lives were ultimately written, in a later generation, there had been so great a lapse of time that the biographers worked in considerable detachment and distance. To this day we have had no satisfactory life of Matthew Arnold, and Gordon Ray's pioneer life of Thackeray became possible only after he assembled a monumental edition of Thackeray's letters. T. S. Eliot, as I write, is being loyally defended by his widow. In spite of her efforts, certain "vulgarly impertinent" biographies have appeared. Henry James was defended by his nephew and executor. He had also taken precautions. He burned his papers in a great bonfire in his garden at Lamb House. Like Dickens, who lit a similar fire at Gad's Hill, he could not burn letters which had reached other's hands. When his nephew died, James's own epistolary genius, like Thackeray's, betrayed him. His life was made possible because thousands of letters had been treasured and saved. We may note that Auden's request in his will, beseeching his friends to burn his letters, is not being scrupulously heeded. To some of them it would seem like burning Auden himself.

The novel, still hardy and in late middle age, seems to have run its course as a form. One wonders whether there is much more to be learned about the craft of fiction, after the experiments of James, Proust, Joyce, Kafka and the *nouveau roman*. In its three centuries, fiction galloped from the epistolary-picaresque to the high-dramatic, through phases we label "romantic-realism" and "naturalism-symbolism." From dealing with the outwardness of things the novel tried to describe "the stream of consciousness"—indulging in angles of vision, simultaneities and spatial form, as if the novel were a camera. But if fiction has, it seems, exhausted experiment, there remains much to be learned about biography. It cannot claim narrative sophistications. It is backward enough still to invoke Boswell as a supreme model, forgetting that not all biographers know their subjects as a living presence. Nor has life-writing developed a freedom of form and structure approximating the novelist's freedoms: and it has not articulated a "methodology." There is a book called *The Craft of Fiction,* but no such useful book exists for biography. By its very nature biography has been wedded always—and always will be—to the document, to fact and anecdote, and certainly to gossip; and it will have to reckon increasingly with the portentous libraries heaped around modern figures. Also, in opposition to the novel, it may not invent conversation. The world does a great deal of talking—but rarely in biographies. This is one of biography's greatest limitations. One of the reaons for the enduring charm and force of Boswell is that he recorded Johnson's words and wit, one suspects accurately, because Boswell himself could not have invented such talk. The tape recorder will be an increasingly useful instrument in providing "oral history" for biographers; but the essential character of the art remains unchanged. A biographer's narrative imagination is fettered by the very nature of his enterprise. He must adhere to fact, so far as fact can be determined. He may be judged by the resourcefulness with which he works within prescribed conditions.

We have reached a moment in literary history when time and circumstance summon biography to declare itself and its principles. Can it take its place as a primary art form? I would like to think so; and it should summon poets and novelists to attempt the form instead of leaving it (in Strachey's phrase) to "journeymen of letters." Biography has been the wayward child of individual talents; it has suffered, through three centuries, from a lack of definition, a laxity of method. The biographical feeling inherent in man which gave us the vignettes and stories of the Old Testament and the lives of Christ, which guided Plutarch to write his fabled narratives making us party to the passions of the ancient world, has culminated in singularly few masterpieces. Buried within the unexplored narrative forms of biography is an urge to charter a human odyssey. The fabulous and the magical, the tales of man as a creative enigma, give way now to the exactitudes of science. And caught up in a technological society, man tends to feel himself increasingly dehumanized; thus he once more reaches for the lives of others to assure himself of the commonalities of existence. Biography, when it dealt with ancient times, could allow itself freedoms of conjecture; the material was thin; much of it was folk tale and the biographer had to make his peace with Michelet's silences—the royal grant of wine accorded Chaucer; Shakespeare's second-best bed. The historian of human lives, in his saturation, could allow himself at best an "educated" guess. Like the architect he might extrapolate columns from fragments. Still, biography has lacked the courage to discover bolder ways of human reconstruction. Our times certainly provide wider latitudes.

What gives strength to biographers is the science of anthropology, the observations of the social sciences, above all the explorations of the individual psyche opened up by Freud. The new "science of man" offers biography a new role in literature and in history. It tells biography that it has for too long grasped the "empirical" and smothered itself too much in externals. There have been too many graveyard lives, the panegyrics Strachey mocked. The celebration of worthies is still considered sufficient—at a moment when there has opened for us new horizons which enable us to use both technology and art in capturing extinct lives. The best counsel Lytton Strachey could give to practitioners was that biography should possess a "becoming brevity": that we should emulate French writers of memoirs and lives, like Fontenelle and Condorcet. These compressed "into a few shining pages the manifold existences of men." Strachey's advice relates principally to craft; yet it implies a great deal of insight into the nature of men *within* their manifold existences. Virginia Woolf wrote more than a dozen brilliant essays on biography. In essence they talked of the struggle between the "granite" of fact and the "rainbow" of fiction. She also wrote a fable for biographers in *Orlando;* and a history of the scent of things when (in her highly imaginative way), she adumbrated a life for Elizabeth Barrett Browning's dog. Having written two imagined biographies, one of an androgynous protean human, who takes varied shapes through the centuries, and the other of a canine, she finally wrote the life of the art critic Roger Fry. Her diaries reveal that she felt harnessed to "fact" while her mind struggled for the freedom of her fancy. If we go back two centuries, we find Boswell, the architect of one kind of modern biography, secure in his intimate knowledge of Dr. Johnson, whom he had observed closely for two decades. He boasted that he would not melt down his materials. He wanted the voice of his subject to be constantly heard. "I cannot conceive," said Boswell, "a more pefect mode of writing any man's life than ... interweaving what he privately wrote, and said, and thought." Splendid, indeed, when one has access to the subject in the flesh! What would Boswell have done with a modern tape recorder: let us imagine him confronting, at the end of twenty years, a house filled with tapes? He would have been forced to melt his materials or be choked by them. Boswell was in any event being ingenuous; his "oral history" had the benefit of condensations from the first. It was imposed by the labor of the tracing pen in the remarkable minutes he kept of Dr. Johnson's aggressive and pungent manner of conversation. No other instrument was available to him. In the very process of writing these minutes (he did not use shorthand) he selected and even at times "melted down" his data. Yet in spite of this, one reviewer complained that Boswell's gold had not been "ingotted."

His doctrine, or the workshop observations of the moderns, hardly constitute a *principia biographica.* Such a *principia,* less formal and scientific than those of mathematics and philosophy, or the anatomies of criticism of our time, might be set down in a modest way. Let us recognize that the explorations of Sigmund Freud and his successors have created a new province for biographical adventure and knowledge, and a new audience eager to study particular kinds of human nature and the motivations of human achievement. We might enunciate certain principles for those increasingly attracted to the recording and telling of human lives. One would be that the writings and utterances of any subject contain more secrets of character and personality than we have hitherto allowed. A life-myth is hidden within every poet's work, and in the gestures of a politician, the canvases and statues of art and the "life-styles" of charismatic characters. Whole "case histories" could be compiled out of revealed experience, out of what human beings "express"—for we understand so much more now about behavior and motivation. In this way we can draw larger conclusions about an inner life, of which the "outer" life is constant expression. Some such principles come to us from the new psychology.

In recognizing that biography is accorded at present a secondary place in literary studies we may note the continuing vogue of what some critics have called "an age of criticism." Biography deals with so much human stuff that the interest of both the critical and lay reader has resided in the materials and not in their form or manner of presentation. When the media speak of the "Nixon story" or "the Patton story," it sounds as if there were only one story to be told. The "New Criticism" would not listen, when the new biography argued that the poet is his poem, the novelist his novel. Criticism, singularly self-centered, refused to understand that a critic is constantly involved not only in his own process, which he regards with such self-absorption and often self-indulgence, but in a biographical process as well. The winds of change can be seen in the curious theorems of critics like Harold Bloom, who uses Freudian generalizations, and splashes about a great deal in biography. In this indirect way such a critic is announcing the belated wedding of biography and criticism; but also of biography and psychology—or—, to put it another way, he announces the gradual awakening of criticism to the fact of an inexorable and undivorceable marriage. Is it not strange that many critics who attempted to write lives have floundered in the archives? They thought of biography only in Boswellian terms; or they felt as if the recital of the classic laundry lists was what biography really is. The critical ego often is so deeply concerned with critical ideas and their justification, that it is incapable of empathy with the vicissitudes of lived lives. So we are now in the process of putting the poet back into his poem after trying to remove him or drown him in floods of critical explication. We are beginning to understand—what historians knew always—that literary history is a record of what happens from the moment an imaginative writer puts pen to paper, or speaks words into an electronic device, or applies his fingers to a typewriter keyboard. The world's curiosity asks more insistently than ever for the humanity of the lived life. It wants to know how poems or stories, paintings or music, politicians or soldiers, came into being. Strange indeed the ways in which poets themselves in popular readings of their words, facing enraptured audiences, have found it expedient to talk of their art, their thoughts, their divorces, their children. The impersonal poet and his impersonal poem disappear. A whole new world of biography has been opened by "confessional poetry." Individuals in our society proclaim their lives from the roof tops. Our greatest problem is to find artists equal to the task of setting them down.

In these jottings for a *principia* I find myself tracing four principles which have been my main theme these many years. I have already suggested two and I will expand them:

The first is that the biographer must learn to understand man's ways of dreaming, thinking and using his fancy. This does not mean that a biographical subject can be psychoanalyzed; a biographical subject is not a patient and not in need of therapy. But there can be found analytic methods applicable to biography in which the subject's fancies, thoughts and dreams are used for the revelations they contain. By an analytic approach to biography I mean the kind of analysis which enables us to see through the rationalizations, the postures, the self-delusions and self-deceptions of our subjects—in a word the manifestations of the unconscious as they are projected in conscious forms of action within whatever walks of life our subject has chosen. The very choice of a given walk of life is in itself revelatory. Such analysis is not learned from reading a book by Freud or Jung or the other writing psychoanalysts of our time. The biographer must first learn to understand his own fancy so as not to confuse it with that of his subject.

This brings me to the second principle—that biographers must struggle constantly not to be taken over by their subjects, or to fall in love with them. The secret of this struggle is to learn to be a participant-observer. A good biography implies a degree of involvement—otherwise the work has little feeling. But there must, at the same time, be a strong grip on the biographical self, so that total disengagement is possible. An empathic feeling need not involve identification. No good biography can be written in total love and admiration; and it is even less useful if it is written in hate. This problem of identification is in reality at the core of modern biography, and it explains some of its most serious failures.

The third principle, which might be an extension of the first, is that a biographer must analyze his materials to discover certain keys to the deeper truths of his subject—keys as I have said to the private mythology of the individual. These belong to the truths of human behavior which modern psychology has extensively explored and which we must assiduously study. This is what I mean when I speak constantly of searching for "the figure under the carpet." By studying first the figure in the carpet—that is the patterns and modes of a man's works, in literature, in politics, in most of his endeavors—we are able then to grasp what lies on the underside of the given tapestry. The public facade is the mask behind which a private mythology is hidden—the private self-concept that guides a given life, the private dreams of the self. In seeking this mythology we use inductive methods as boldly as a detective uses deductive. The ways in which men and women handle their lives, the forms they give to their acts of living, their particular forms of sexual politics for example, their handling of human relations, their ways of wooing the world or disdaining it—all this is germane to biography, it is the very heart of a biography. The mythological keys help guide us through the mazes of modern archives. But we must also recognize that, while the mythological configuration is more or less determined, there are cases in which we find ego development and ego change. We are, however, constantly involved with determinism.

My fourth and perhaps final principle relates to form and structure. Every life takes its own form and a biographer must find the ideal and unique literary form that will express it. In structure a biography need no longer be strictly chronological, like a calendar or datebook. Lives are rarely lived in that way. An individual repeats patterns learned in childhood, and usually moves forward and backward through memory. Proust is perhaps a better guide to modern biography than Boswell.

In sum I would say that my four principles—and doubtless others will come up (these are but starting points)—suggest that a constant struggle is waged between a biographer and his subject, a struggle between the concealed self and the revealed self, the public self and the private. And the task and duty of biographical narrative is to sort out themes and patterns, not dates and mundane calendar events which sort themselves. This can be accomplished by use of those very devices that have given narrative strength to fiction—flashbacks, retrospective chapters, summary chapters, jumps from childhood to maturity, glimpses of the future, forays into the past— that is the way we live and move; art can be derived from this knowledge.

Let these four principles stand as my view of some of the foundations of the New Biography: the biography we have been creating since the days of Lytton Strachey. He was the first to use Freud in a constructive manner—although he used him *en amateur* and at second-hand. I would add finally that a biographer who does not possess a literary style and the ability to be concise and clear, had better shut up shop. Brilliant lives have been dulled by dull biographers; and dull lives have at times been rendered brilliant in the same process. A singular part of our quest is a quest for proportion. A life must be shaped, but not distorted or made subject of the biographer's eye. The integrity and intensity of the biographer's process, and his ways of proceeding, usually shine through his work. He is far from anonymous. He is present in his work as the portrait painter is present in his. And he stands or falls by the amount of confidence or of distrust he creates in the reader. If he is absent from the work, his book is usually a flabby performance, lacking force and heart.

Let me add as a possible subject the question of biographical criticism. There exists, I am sorry to say, no criticism of biography worthy of the name. Reviewers and critics have learned how to judge plays, poems, novels—but they reveal their helplessness in the face of a biography. They reflect their uncertainty about the facts, which they can't immediately verify, and so they discuss their own interest in the details or gossip of a life rather than in the art of representation which a biography must be—and it is this art which is truly their concern. Biographers are left with only one course: to teach critics how to read a biography with proper judicial awareness even if the critic doesn't know the archive. How has the biographer distinguished between his reliable and unreliable witnesses? How has he avoided making himself simply the voice of his subject? How has he told his story? Does the data produced justify itself in the narrative? These questions are answerable in the reading of any biography. Up to the present, biography has been an art little aware of itself and mixed up too much with *ad hoc* rules of thumb, personal superstitions and personal prejudices. We are at the beginning of our journey.

Dilemmas

LYTTON STRACHEY described biography as "the most delicate and humane of all the branches of the art of writing." Delicate, because the biographer seeks to restore a sense of life to the inert materials that survive an individual's passage on this earth—seeks to recapture some part of what was once tissue and brain, and above all, feeling, and to shape a likeness of the vanished figure. Humane, because inevitably the biographical process is a refining, a civilizing—a humanizing—process. And because it is a delicate and humane process, it partakes of all the ambiguities and contradictions of life itself. A biography is a record, in words, of something that is as mercurial and as flowing, as compact of temperament and emotion, as the human spirit itself.

The writer of biography must be neat and orderly and logical in describing this elusive flamelike human spirit which delights in defying order and neatness and logic. The biographer may be as imaginative as he pleases—the more imaginative the better—in the way in which he brings together his materials, *but he must not imagine the materials.* He must read himself into the past; but he must also read the past into the present. He must judge the facts, but he must not sit in judgment. He must respect the dead—but he must tell the truth.

James Anthony Froude sought to tell the truth about the Carlyles and succeeded in bringing down upon his writing table all the hornets of literary London—and of Edinburgh to boot. And yet while he was doing this, other Victorians were being commemorated in large, heavy tomes; they were made to seem not men, but angels, clothed in the purity of Adam before the Fall. The biographers who offered the public such gilded statues were considered honorable and truthful men. But candor such as Froude's provoked indignation and, indeed, fright. We deal here in large anomalies.

It is my intention to focus in particular on a specialized branch of biography—the writing of the lives of men and women who were themselves writers. Obviously all the practices and traditions of biography apply to this kind of biographical writing: the differences between it and other categories reside essentially in the nature of the subject and corollary questions of emphasis and shading. The biographer of a soldier is apt to be concerned with such matters as strategy and military discipline, the qualities of the military mind, a life of movement and action, indeed all the historic forces that enter into play when we put a soldier into the field. The biographer of a poet is likely to be concerned with literary rather than military discipline, that is, with literary criticism and with the life of the imagination in action. But all biography has this in common, that it is concerned with the truth of life and the truth of experience. How far can a biographer, who by force of circumstances is always outside his subject (and sometimes decades and centuries removed from it), penetrate into the subject's mind, and obtain insights which are not vouchsafed him even in the case of his most intimate friends? What is the essence of a life, and how do we disengage that essence from the eternal clutter of days and years, the inexorable tick of the clock—and yet restore the sense of that very tick? Which are the true witnesses of this or that life and which the false? And how shall a life be written? What style will best render the existence of an individual who had some style of his own? And how tell, in especial, the life of the mind, which is what the literary life really is:—the mind and the emotions—as distinct from the lives of generals and politicians whose intellectual attainments were not written out day after day upon sheets of paper in a study, but were lived out in Parliament or on the battlefield?

I propose to offer, first, certain general considerations about the biographer and his subject, and to proceed thereafter to discuss the quest for materials—the plunge into archives, that constant search for significant detail, much of it irrecoverable, which is half the passion of the biographer and which must occur before he can put pen to paper. And then we must weigh the relationship between criticism and biography, for surely the writing of a literary life would be nothing but a kind of indecent curiosity, and an invasion of privacy, were it not that it seeks always to illuminate, insofar as possible, the mysterious and magical process of creation. That process belongs to the inner consciousness, those deeper springs of our being where the gathered memories of our lives merge and in some cases are distilled into transcendent art. To understand this we can, in our time, invoke the aid of psychology. But we must ask ourselves—how useful is Freud to the biographer, to what extent may he be invoked?

Finally it will be fruitful to consider closely the relationship the biographer must establish between himself and those clocks which rang the hours in other years.

[35

Writing lives involves us in the consideration of the entire life process.

It is not my intention to venture into the history of biography. It would take us too far afield. There is much to say about the deeply human biographical narratives of the Gospels and their exalted subject; or about the vivid biographical paragraphs in the Old Testament, so evocative in their brevity, devoted to Ruth and David and Joseph; or about Plutarch, who was concerned with the writing of great lives for the valued ethical generalizations they might yield him in his comparisons of the noble Greeks and Romans. It would be tempting to deal also with the hagiographers, who in their lives of the saints made little claim to science and often even less to veracity, but freely transposed, on occasion, episodes from the life of one saint to another. What was important for them was the example of the saintly life not the facts of the life itself. My concern here is not with history or with biographies remote in time from us, and so rich a part of our religious and secular heritage. The problem I wish to discuss is the very concrete one of how, in modern times, when we have whole libraries of documents, when tape recorders and films bring to us the voice and the image of the biographical subject—how, in these modern times, biography should be written, and by what, light we are to work. Can we enunciate a *principia biographica?*

Interest in the private life of the man of letters dates in English literature from the curiosity and zeal of Izaak Walton (though earlier precursors might be found) who between 1640 and 1678 wrote biographies of Donne, Sir Henry Wotton, Richard Hooker, George Herbert and Robert Saunderson. These were published as Walton's

Lives. To this same period belong the important minutes of lives written by John Aubrey and Fuller's *History of the Worthies of England.* Some of these works were influenced by North's translation of Plutarch. The Elizabethan world had invested its supreme passions in the greatness of England, as Shakespeare's histories attest. There had been, however, scant interest in personal history and in the preservation of the literary remains of individuals. In this sense the publication of the First Folio of Shakespeare was not only an act of preservation of our richest and greatest literary inheritance. It was a profoundly biographical act. What followed, logically enough, was an interest in the greatness of Englishmen as well as in England. And in the United States, after the colonial period, the importance of the individual, especially in the full tide of the romantic movement, inaugurated the celebration of the lives of notable men and women—the founding fathers quite naturally coming first.

The interest in the personal and the private life, the life of the inner man, dates in English letters, we might say, from the eighteenth century: certainly it was a harbinger of romanticism. First came the poet, and very much later curiosity about the life of the poet. Had biographical curiosity, or awareness, existed earlier, we would not today be trying to piece together Chaucer's life from those paltry records of his pension and the pitchers of wine bestowed upon him by the royal household. Who would think of writing the life of a modern poet from the record of his check stubs? We write what we pretend is a "life" of Shakespeare from a series of facts which can be set down in a very large hand on a rather small sheet of paper. The Elizabethans kept no record of the luminous mind in their midst; yet so great is our curiosity that, failing an adequate biography of Shakespeare, certain individuals give him a wholly new life and call him Bacon or the Earl of Oxford.

Readers of novels often ask novelists how they came to write their works. Poetry readings are almost epidemic in our time. There is no comparable interest in biography as a creative endeavor. Readers of biographies tend to take for granted the facts given them; they do not seem to be aware that there has been an act of composition. They think of biographies as being like photographs, "documentary." For this reason we have had few treatises on the writing of lives such as offered us by Lubbock or Forster for fiction. This is a pity because during the 1920s, under the fertilizing influence of Lytton Strachey, many voices were heard, and the foundations of the New Biography were laid. There were Harold Nicolson and André Maurois, and chiming in we had the voices of Strachey himself and of his friend Virginia Woolf and the group of younger men who learned from them—among them Lord David Cecil and Philip Guedalla. Nicolson reluctantly saw biography as doomed to become a work of science, Maurois argued it could be only an art and should accept itself as such and Virginia Woolf said it was neither art nor science but a kind of superior *craft*.

Nicolson's survey, which tended to be rather sketchy as history, was in reality an essay in definition. He saw biography as "the history of the lives of individual men as a branch of literature" but gloomily predicted that it would eventually become a kind of laboratory project. He was writing under the influence of the first popularizations of psychoanalysis fifty years ago and such ephemeral fads as the transplanting of monkey glands. He believed that biographies would tend increasingly to be case histories rather than lives related in literary form. He wrote:

> I would suggest that the scientific interest in biography is hostile to, and will in the end prove destructive of, the literary interest. The former will insist not only on the facts, but on all the facts; the latter demands a partial or artificial representation of facts. The scientific interest, as it develops, will become insatiable; no synthetic power, no genius for representation, will be able to keep pace. I foresee, therefore, a divergence between the two interests. Scientific biography will become specialised and technical. There will be biographies in which psychological development will be traced in all its intricacy and in a manner comprehensible only to the experts; there will be biographies examining the influence of heredity—biographies founded on Galton, on Lombroso, on Havelock Ellis, on Freud; there will be medical biographies—studies of the influence on character of the endocrine glands, studies of internal secretions; there will be sociological biographies, economic biographies, aesthetic biographies, philosophical biographies. These will doubtless be interesting and instructive, but the emphasis which will be thrown on the analytical or scientific aspect will inevitably lessen the literary effort applied to their composition. The more that biography becomes a branch of science the less will it become a branch of literature.

Now that we have lived a bit into this future, we can see that Nicolson's forebodings, for the time being at least, were groundless. There have been some specialized biographies of the sort he envisaged; their public is limited and they certainly have not supplanted traditional biography. Biographers have continued to write, fully aware, as André Maurois insisted, that man is volatile. Indeed so long as the brain and nerves and human conditionings defy mechanization, biography cannot claim to be scientific. But there is no reason why it should not aspire to certain scientific methods and use, where relevant, computers and other technological aids.

Our discussion is focused on how to use available knowledge rather than argue about art versus science. Biography is an art when the work is composed, brought together, given structure, form and narrative style. It becomes documentary when it is a compendium—that is not composed, but merely assembled in some kind of chronological order, without a particular theory of selection and a code of relevance. These are tolerably obvious matters. Biography must learn that it is not an intellectual process alone; it has to deal with emotions and to discover the emotional content of some of its material. All biographers neglect an entire province of study and illumination if they neglect modern psychology and its findings. Psychology alone can help turn the baser metals of fact, the crude verbosity of documents, into the gold of human personality.

To succeed the biographer must perform the unusual—and the well-nigh impossible—act of incorporating into himself the experience of another, or shall we say, becoming for a while that other person, even while remaining himself. This does not mean that he must be an actor. The actor is a role player; he gets into the skin of a character and remains that character on stage, wholly dissimulating his real self. The biographer also is required to get into the skin of his subject; he removes himself sometimes to another age; sometimes he even changes his sex; he takes on another's career, the very wink of an eye or shrug of a shoulder: yet all the while he retains his own mind, his own sense of balance and his own appraising glance. Biographers must be warm, yet aloof, involved, yet uninvolved. To be cold as ice in appraisal, yet warm and human and understanding, this is the biographer's dilemma.

Boswell

LET US IMAGE the great table of biography—for biographers need larger tables or desks than most writers. It is piled high with books and papers: certificates of birth and death, genealogies, photos of deeds, letters—letters filled with rationalizations and subterfuges, exaggerations, wishful thinking, deliberate falsehoods, elaborate politenesses—and then, testimonials, photographs, manuscripts, diaries, notebooks, bank checks, newspaper clippings, as if we had poured out the contents of desk drawers or of old boxes in an attic: a great chaotic mass of materials, not to forget volumes of memoirs by contemporaries—how they abound in some cases!—and the diaries and notebooks of these contemporaries, and often biographies of the subject written by other hands. All this material, assembled out of the years, will make its way into the mind—and the heart—of the person who has gathered it. The death of the owner of many of these documents has tended to level them into a relative uniformity. We can no longer determine whether this particular letter, breathing sweetness and affection, was really written in love, or in pretense of love. The voice that gave it its original inflection is gone; the recipient of the letter is perhaps no longer available to furnish a gloss or to testify what it meant to receive it. Things impalpable surround these palpable objects. The diaries and notes reflecting moods ranging from vexation and anger to transcendent joy, bitter animosiy to boundless Christian charity, all had a particular meaning when the author was alive. The biographer can only absorb these documents into his living consciousness: it becomes, for the time, surrogate for the consciousness that has been extinguished. In other words, the living, associating, remembering biographer's mind seeks to restore a time sense to the mass of data that has become timeless. "The dead," said Joseph Conrad, "can live only with the exact intensity and quality of the life imparted to them by the living." All biography is, in effect, a reprojection into words, into a literary or a kind of semiscientific and historical form, of the inert materials, reassembled, so to speak, through the mind of the historian or the biographer. His becomes the informing mind. He can only lay bare the facts as he has understood them, in a continuous and inquiring narrative.

I

Henry James set down some very eloquent words on this subject—of the change that takes place between the moment when a man is alive, holding the thousands of connecting threads that bind him to the world and his fellow men, and the moment when the threads are snapped, for all time. "After a man's long work is over and the sound of his voice is still," wrote James, "those in whose regard he has held a high place find his image strangely simplified and summarized. The hand of death, in passing over it, has smoothed the folds, made it more typical and general. The figure retained by memory is compressed and intensified; accidents have dropped away from it and shades have ceased to count; it stands, sharply, for a few estimated and cherished things, rather than, nebulously, for a swarm of possibilities." There is indeed an extraordinary simplification, and the life that was so rich, so full of countless moments of experience and emotion, now is disconnected and fragmentary. Let us place Henry James's words in their proper context. The novelist was writing of his lately dead friend, James Russell Lowell. When he set down these words it was with the image of Lowell in his mind, as he had known him during more than three decades. The beautiful commemorative essay that he wrote gives us a vision of many Lowells—the Lowell to whom James had listened when he was a young man at Harvard, listened during late winter afternoons when lamps were lit in the classroom and they illuminated the bearded face, giving to it a haunted poetic quality; the vigorous American Lowell in Paris during the 1870's with whom James supped at a little hotel on the Left Bank before crossing the Seine, illumined by gaslight which gave to the water the effect of a varnishd surface, to go to the Théâtre Français; the Lowell of the earlier time who set down noble lines in memory of the dead, the young dead, of the American Civil War; and the later Lowell, the man of letters-as-diplomat, carrying the responsibilities of his ministerial post to the Court of St. James's and into the great houses of Victorian England, the Lowell who lectured the English on the growth of democracy in America. The "estimated and cherished things" were those estimated and cherished by James at the time of Lowell's death in 1891. Yet we, from our distance, a century later, and many years after James's death, find that time has further summarized and distanced Lowell. A certain staleness pervades his writings—they seem bookish and derivative; he has stepped into a greater shadow; at moments he seems to us, in our twentieth-century sophistication, a figure naïve and parochial; he *lives* for us vividly only in some of his essays and lectures and largely when a writer, like James, succeeds in making him vivid for us. What James wrote, in turn, has become one more document—a very beautiful document—one more bit of eloquent testimony to be placed upon the already burdened table of Lowell's biography. The figure of James, along with other of Lowell's contemporaries, has moved into the records of Lowell's life; and the biographer, his task more complex than ever, must himself move among these shadows and documents and "points of view," called upon to sift, to evaluate, to recreate. His task grows in magnitude when he encounters, and places upon his worktable, biographies of his subject written by his predecessors. Here we find we must make still further distinctions—distinctions not often made—between the biographer who writes solely from documents and the one who writes, frequently from a commemorative emotion, having known the dead man. This, very properly, brings us to the name and the example of James Boswell.

II

What sort of man was Boswell? We can see him in Frederick A. Pottle's life in all his contradictory phases. As might be expected from the chief editor of Yale's massive Boswell archive, Professor Pottle's work is substantial and authoritative. His story is the fruit of a long saturation in the copious yield of Fettercairn and Malahide. By now the details of Boswell's compulsive haunting of brothels and his pursuit of the great are well known. Pottle addresses himself, as a biographer should, to the character and personality of his subject, and enables us to attempt an answer to the riddle propounded long ago by Macaulay: how was it possible for this eighteenth century provincial, a rake and a buffoon, to make a progress to the high places of literature? How could Boswell, the busybody who held himself in such low esteem, have written the life of Johnson?

If this riddle was Victorian and was cogently answered by Carlyle, it is still a good psychological riddle. We can see the paradox with many refinements of detail. Pottle begins with an unpublished autobiographical sketch by Boswell written for Rousseau—a confession by the young boisterous Scot to the master confessor of the century. In it, the twenty-four-year-old Boswell describes how as a boy he suffered from the wrathful God of Calvinism and the effects of a mother "extremely kind but too anxious." He blames her for frightening him early with "the eternity of punishment." Boswell omits his fear of his stern father, the Laird of Auchinleck. Indeed Boswell speaks of his father as "worthy" and as "one of the ablest and worthiest men in the world"; he thereby witholds from Rousseau the truth of his chronic quarrels with his parent. "You will see in me," he adds, "an extraordinary example of the effects of a bad education." Perhaps he is thinking of Rousseau's *Émile*.

The bad education was distinctly in the realm of the emotions. His father sat in judgment at home as he did on the bench; and between religious and paternal wrath, the spirited boy had little choice. James Boswell found it politic to be constantly ill. As he matured, a kind tutor and two college friends (oddly enough, one was named Johnston and the other's middle name was Johnson) gave him the confidence to substitute rebellion for illness. At first this took forms of fantasy. He wished to go to

America. He sought to join the Guards. Above all he committed the religio-political sin of flirting with Catholicism. The dissolute Lord Eglinton resolved these issues. Pottle tells us that he "rescued Boswell from religious error by making him a libertine."

The accepted modern opinion has been that Boswell engaged in a life-long "search for a father" and that Johnson's mixture of curmudgeonry and affection supplied the want. But Boswell's relation to authority was in reality more complex. We can discern his cycles of rebellion, his ever-present feeling of guilt—his sense, from earliest childhood, of his worthlessness. This led to a great deal of self-surveillance with constant relapses into self-indulgence and various modes of self-punishment. Pottle argues convincingly that Boswell's recklessly acquired venereal infections may have been one way of imposing sufferings of the flesh. They also provided for periods of abstinence and a feeling of re-established virtue. Another form of self-punishment may have been Boswell's regular attendance at executions, a form of self-punishment and, of mental suicide. The executions gave him terrible nightmares. They also ministered to his ability to be cruel and masochistic. It was always as if he were attending his own execution.

He found relief in diaries and journals which he kept regularly. He could catechize himself in these as if he were his father. He could vent his spleen. He could confess to himself, and secretly to the world. His condensed notations would be banal enough save that suddenly there is a flash, an insight, as if he recognizes himself in his word-mirror. "Desperate. This day, *Easter,* rouse. Be Johnson!" He consoles himself: "You've done no harm. Be *retenu."* And suddenly: "What am I?" What indeed! This last might have been asked by a character in Kafka.

When Boswell forced himself on Rousseau or Voltaire or Paoli, or when he knelt for Johnson's blessing, he seems to have been piecing together a personality for himself out of the lives of the famous. The biography of Johnson will in the end be also a biography of Boswell.

Parallel with his excesses in theatres, where he publicly clowned (he liked to do barnyard imitations before the plays began), his taking prostitutes in the streets and foul alleyways of London, we have his earnest—but in reality half-hearted—quest for a wife. The celebrated courtship of the bluestocking Belle de Zuylen was told by Geoffrey Scott with irony and economy in his *Portrait of Zélide*.

Boswell always skillfully sabotaged his wooings. No "lover" could have been clumsier and more unfeeling, perhaps because his gallantries masked a contempt for women. He was nearly always ready to buy the cheapest kind of love, even when he had kindly, maternal mistresses. When he finally married, it was in haste and to a first cousin. He unbachelored himself, it seems, more in anger than in love, as if to match his father's remarriage. The weddings were on the same day.

At twenty-nine the young Boswell had won a show of fame with his book on Corsica. He had published appalling verses; he seemed more a precursor of press-agentry and public relations than of biographical literature. Certainly there is something third-rate in the Boswell of these years. However his journals, written originally for himself in privacy, are remarkable. Anyone who has tried to write fiction and keep a journal knows the important difference—a journal does not require a novelist's imagination. Yet Boswell had a method. He taught himself the secrets of recording and self-documentation. He experimented, says Pottle, "and discarded until his infallible sense of tune picked up the precise unifying notes." It is always by their unifying notes that a biography becomes a work of art.

The unifying note in the life of James Boswell was his meeting with Samuel Johnson.

III

When Boswell began his preparations to write the life of Samuel Johnson, that ponderous figure still walked at large and London still echoed to his conversation and opinions. Boswell was in a position of high advantage. Johnson believed that "nobody can write the life of a man but those who have eat and drunk and lived in social intercourse with him." This was a superficial statement, but what biographer, in Johnson's company, would discourage its geniality, its claim that intimacy breeds knowledge when it might breed contempt, or distortion, or even certain kinds of psychological blindness. Certainly not Boswell, who was ready to eat, drink, live and worship Johnson. He could listen. He could take notes. He could ask questions.

He could do much more. He could at moments become a kind of organizer and sceneshifter in the life of Dr. Johnson: he could create occasions, incidents, encounters for the life he would ultimately write. This is not to say that he actually arranged Johnson's life for him. The learned doctor was, intellectually, the least passive of men. There were moments, however, when Boswell could, by quiet manipulation, place his subject in a better position for the biographical camera, improve a little on the accidents of life; he could carefully plan— shall we say?—"spontaneous" occasions for the unaware object of his biographical urge. What is disarming in the life he finally wrote, is the candor and innocence with which Boswell describes his own maneuvers and cleverness. There comes to mind the little episode of the visit to the home of the late Reverend Edward Young, the celebrated author of *Night Thoughts on Life, Death and Immortality*. Johnson was traveling with Boswell and they stopped at Welwyn, where Young had been rector for more than a quarter of a century. The celebrity-loving, pilgrimage-seeking Boswell wanted to visit the Young house, where the poet's son now lived; and he wanted to do it *with* Dr. Johnson. He feared, however, that Johnson might refuse. Let us see how he goes about his little project:

> We stopped at Welwyn, where I wished much to see, in company with Dr. Johnson, the residence of the authour of *Night Thoughts,* which was then possessed by his son, Mr. Young. Here some address was requisite, for I was not acquainted with Mr. Young, and had I proposed to Dr. Johnson that we should send to him, he would have checked my wish, and perhaps been offended. I therefore concerted with Mr. Dilly [their companion on the journey] that I should steal away from Dr. Johnson and him, and try what reception I could procure from Mr. Young; if unfavourable, nothing was to be said; but if agreeable, I should return and notify it to them. I hastened to Mr. Young's, found he was at home, sent in word that a gentleman desired to wait upon him, and was shewn into a parlour, where he and a young lady, his daughter, were sitting. He appeared to be a plain, civil, country gentleman; and when I begged pardon for presuming to trouble him, but that I wished much to see his place, if he would give me leave; he behaved very courteously, and answered, "By all means, Sir; we are just going to drink tea; will you sit down?" I thanked him, but

said, that Dr. Johnson had come with me from London, and I must return to the inn and drink tea with him; that my name was Boswell, I had travelled with him in the Hebrides. "Sir, (said he,) I should think it a great honour to see Dr. Johnson here. Will you allow me to send for him?" Availing myself of this opening, I said that "I would go myself and bring him, when he had drunk tea; he knew nothing of my calling here." Having been thus successful, I hastened back to the inn, and informed Dr. Johnson that "Mr. Young, son of Dr. Young, the authour of *Night Thoughts,* whom I had just left, desired to have the honour of seeing him at the house where his father lived." Dr. Johnson luckily made no inquiry how this invitation had arisen, but agreed to go, and when we entered Mr. Young's parlour, he addressed him with a very polite bow, "Sir, I had a curiosity to come and see this place. I had the honour to know that great man, your father." We went into the garden, where we found a gravel walk, on each side of which was a row of trees, planted by Dr. Young, which formed a handsome Gothick arch. Dr. Johnson called it a fine grove. I beheld it with reverence.

The scene has been set, the visit arranged. Boswell now can listen to Johnson discourse upon the subject of Dr. Young. The insatiably curious Bozzy has, for the occasion at least, satisfied his curiosity and succeeded in his stratagem. The learned doctor seems to enjoy himself; the deception has been harmless enough. And the episode illustrates the striking advantages an energetic biographer can enjoy when he is master not only of documents but of living situations, and when his subject is within easy and friendly reach.

But Boswell not only set his living scenes; he often gave direction to the conversation within them. He was free, indeed, to discuss even the subject of biography with his biographical subject.

Talking of biography, I said, in writing a life, a man's peculiarities should be mentioned, because they mark his character. *Johnson.* "Sir, there is no doubt as to peculiarities: the question is, whether a man's vices should be mentioned; for instance, whether it should be mentioned that Addison and Parnell drank too freely: for people will probably more easily indulge in drinking from knowing this; so that more ill may be done by the example, than good by telling the whole truth."

And Boswell goes on to attempt to reconcile this view with an opposite view expressed by Johnson on another occasion.

Here was an instance of his varying from himself in talk; for when Lord Hailes and he sat one morning calmly conversing in my house at Edinburgh, I well remember that Dr. Johnson maintained that "If a man is to write *A Panegyrick,* he must keep vices out of sight; but if he professes to write *A Life,* he must represent it really as it was:" and when I objected to the danger of telling that Parnell drank to excess, he said, that "it would produce an instructive caution to avoid drinking, when it was seen, that even the learning and genius of Parnell could be debased by it." And in the Hebrides he maintained, as appears from my *Journal,* that a man's intimate friend should mention his faults, if he writes his life.

I cannot take seriously Johnson's "varying from himself in talk"—Boswell's graceful euphemism for contradicting himself—to which the biographer makes allusion. It gives an impression of the play, back and forth, of an active mind, and perhaps even of tongue in cheek. We cannot know when Johnson used a tone of irony; we can no longer catch the precise inflection of his voice; and I am not at all certain that Boswell, ingenious and clever though he was, was always capable of catching *tone.* But we do know that whatever he may have said in his conversations, Johnson insisted emphatically in his writings upon truth and upon psychological insight in the handling of biography. "There are many," he wrote in the *Idler* of 24 November 1759, "who think it an act of piety to hide the faults and failings of their friends, even when they can no longer suffer by detection." And he added, "If we owe regard to the memory of the dead, there is yet more respect to be laid to knowledge, to virtue and to truth." Johnson followed his own counsel in his *Lives of the Poets,* perhaps with an excess of idiosyncrasy and sometimes a want of critical judgment. But it is easy to forgive him, for he strikes a blow for biographical truth. "A blade of grass is always a blade of grass," Johnson told Mrs. Thrale; "men and women are *my* subjects of inquiry."

Boswell set scenes; he sometimes set the course of the conversation; and he boasted openly and truthfully that he made the life of his man of letters more lively, and therefore ultimately more readable:

In the evening we had a large company in the drawing-room, several ladies, the Bishop of Killaloe, Dr. Percy, Mr. Chamberlayne, of the Treasury, &c. &c. Somebody said the life of a mere literary man could not be very entertaining. *Johnson.* "But it certainly may. This is a remark which has been made, and repeated, without justice; why should the life of a literary man be less entertaining than the life of any other man? Are there not as interesting varieties in such a life? As a *literary life* it may be very entertaining."

Boswell. "But it must be better surely, when it is diversified with a little active variety—such as his having gone to Jamaica; or—his having gone to the Hebrides."

"Johnson," adds Boswell after this flattering—and self-flattering—allusion to the tour of which *he* was the chief architect, "was not displeased at this."

And so we can see how Boswell helped to *live* the biography he was ultimately to write; it was he who, on occasion, introduced that "little active variety" into the career of the literary man he had chosen as his subject— or as the mirror to his own prodigious vanity? For we might ask, as we read on, where, in this amazing work, does biography begin and autobiography end? We have seen how Boswell managed to be both behind the scenes and within the talk, genially and busily intrusive, ubiquitous friend, ubiquitous biographer. Perhaps intrusive does not sufficiently describe his Johnsonian activities, for we know that on one occasion, when he was cross-examining a third person about Johnson—and in Johnson's company—the doctor became understandably impatient. "You have but two subjects," he thundered at Boswell, "yourself and me. I am sick of both."

There was, for instance, their little journey undertaken early in 1776. On page after page Boswell gives us those fine everyday details which make Johnson come alive for us at every turn. Yet there are moments, such as when Boswell suddenly begins to have anxieties about his family in London, which, strictly speaking, have nothing to do with the life of Johnson. Boswell tells us: "I enjoyed the luxury of our approach to London, the metropolis which we both loved so much, for the high and varied intellectual pleasure which it furnishes"— and the inimitable Bozzy here makes us pause. We wonder: is Boswell traveling with Johnson or Johnson with Boswell? He adds: "I experienced immediate happiness while whirled along with such a companion." We do not, indeed, begrudge Boswell his happiness so long as he keeps his companion in sight; and we are happy enough to be in presence of his ebullient self. But a biographer, coming upon the scene more than a century later, finds that he must ride in the coach not only with the subject but with the former biographer! Indeed, the former biographer, in more instances than can be counted, manages to step squarely in front of his subject.

When death finally ended the busy life of Dr. Johnson, his disciple, friend, companion, admirer set down his monumental record from a vast long-gathered archive, documentary and reminiscential. Boswell wrote out of close observation; he wrote also from records, as we have seen, sometimes deliberately created—mirrors deliberately held up to catch the reflection of the living Johnson.

IV

We know now that Boswell floundered a great deal in the writing. He appealed for help; he was assisted by Edmond Malone, the eminent scholar of the time. The work did not come easily or spontaneously. In Boswell's mind, Johnson stood too near him as preceptor and dogmatist: he could not write a sentence without some inner quaver that Johnson might not be approving. It was Malone who revised, read the proofs, and annotated four later editions.

This was how the first great modern biography came into being. Harold Nicolson has very happily contrasted biography before and after Boswell as the difference between a series of studio portraits (or a succession of lantern slides) and the cinema. "Boswell," Nicolson said, "invented actuality; he discovered and perfected a biographical formula in which the narrative could be fused with the pictorial, in which the pictorial in its turn could be rendered in a series of photographs so vividly, and, above all, so rapidly, projected as to convey an impression of continuity, of progression—in a word, of life." But we must observe that Boswell was aided in his invention of actuality in biography because Dr. Johnson was *actual* to him. For the fact remains that he did know his subject for twenty-one of his seventy-five years; and while it has been estimated that during these twenty-one years, representing one third of the adult life, he was in Johnson's company on two hundred and seventy-six days, or less than one year, he nevertheless knew a palpable Dr. Johnson; and he knew other persons who knew a palpable Dr. Johnson. He had access not only to his subject but to the subject's wide circle of friends. If he invented actuality, he in some ways invented, or "created," Dr. Johnson as well; or if that be too extreme a way of putting it, let us say that he created lively stage sets and adroit stage directions for the drama he was to write. His book speaks for his power and his assertiveness as a biographer; at the same time he has committed his successors to shifting from point of view to point of view, not only coping with the subject, but puzzling out a large series of mirror images, some with as many distortions as the mirrors in a fun house at a fair. He is the supreme genius of English biography. But he has also been for too long the sole model. We must remember as model he is mainly a guide to those who write the lives of the living. It is quite another matter to write the lives of the dead.

The biographer who works from life, as Boswell did, has an extraordinary advantage over the biographer who works from the document, whether he plays sceneshifter or not. He has seen his man in the flesh, he has been aware of a three-dimensional being, drawing breath and sitting in the midst of an age they both share. In his mind he retains a sharp image of his subject. He has heard the voice and seen the gesture (and even in our age no recording, no cinema picture can provide a substitute for that). The latecoming biographer hears only the rustle of the pages amid the silence of the tomb. This is explanation enough for the fact that the greatest biographies in our literature have been those which were written by men who knew their subjects and who painted them as the painter paints his picture—within a room, a street, a landscape, with a background and a context rich with its million points of contemporaneous attachment. Boswell, Froude, Lockhart, Forster, repose upon our shelves with vividness and mass and authority which later biographers cannot possess.

But the later biographers have quite an opposite advantage, that of greater objectivity gained from wider perspective, their time distance which Sir Max Beerbohm so comfortably described in his lecture on Lytton Strachey: "the past is a work of art, free from irrelevancies and loose ends . . . the dullards have all disappeared. . . . Everything is settled. There's nothing to be done about it—nothing but to contemplate it and blandly form theories about this or that aspect of it." The biographers who knew their subjects in life began with a certain picture of the man they had known; they had a conception of his personality and an image to which documents might be fitted. The documents might, in some cases, alter the image for them, but this does not change the fact that in recreating it they shuttled from life to the document and then from the document to life. The biographer of the long-dead subject shuttles from one document to another: he begins and he ends with his documents. He is obliged to spend much of his time in trying to form, in his mind, that image which his predecessor possessed, so to speak, "ready-made." He labors to visualize its aspect, its style, its manners. Not having the testimony of his own eyes, he finds he must use the testimony of others; and then he discovers that the testimony is often contradictory and invariably colored by individual points of view. But again, precisely this awareness of contradictions may give the distant biographer a marked advantage in his search for the truest picture.

There is then always this peculiar relationship between any biographer and his subject. The biographer undertakes to capture—or to recapture—mirror images, and he must be careful not to reflect a subject in a mirror which is too much himself. Long before he will have to indulge in this dual analysis of subject and self, he must discover the materials out of which his biography will be written. They must be gathered in a strange and often compulsive quest upon which every biographer embarks with a single-mindedness which makes him look into every book index for the mention of his subject and keeps him browsing endlessly in libraries. He enters a labyrinth, the exit of which he cannot know. At the beginning his great worktable is comparatively bare. Long before he has emerged from the maze it will be cluttered with more material than he can ever use; or it may remain so bare that he has virtually no story to tell—save a tale of general bafflement.

Subject

DR. JOHNSON's *Lives of the Poets,* as Boswell tells us, was written at the urging of the London booksellers. They had their fingers on the public's pulse: they knew their readers' curiosity about poetic lives, and their desire for authoritative criticism and judgment. Johnson was approached. Money was offered. A list of poets was furnished. The edition was to be uniform, elegant, widely advertised. The great man was asked to name his price and he modestly asked for £200. All this made Boswell uneasy. His hero was selling himself cheap. Boswell was "somewhat disappointed" that Johnson did not take charge of the undertaking, especially that "he was to furnish a Preface and a Life to any poet the booksellers pleased." Asked Boswell, with his genial tactlessness (which usually charmed Johnson), would the doctor "do this thing to any dunce's works, if they should ask him?" Johnson's famous answer, prompt and professional, was, "Yes, sir, and *say* he was a dunce."

Dr. Johnson was saying in effect that any professional writer of lives and any critic of poetry can set his mind to work on any subject if he wishes—so long as the truth is told. Boswell's question, however, had deeper soundings than even Boswell knew. Having himself selected a biographical subject, out of love and admiration, he could not imagine a biographer choosing any Tom, Dick or Harry. His question (if we look at it more closely) lies at the heart of the biographical enterprise.

In a world of subjects—centuries crowded with notables and dunces—we may indeed ask why a modern biographer fixes his attention on certain faces and turns his back on others. Not all biographers are as democratic as the learned doctor—and even he was choosing poets, not plebeians. Why this particular countenance? What game of probability is being played? There is inevitably some attraction, some choice. Yet to pursue this question is like asking why two people fall in love. Something in the lives of each, some element in their deeper sensibilities, brings into play the strange and mysterious forces of friendship and affection. André Maurois asked himself once why he chose to write a fictional life of Shelley at the beginning of his career. His lame answer was that he wanted to "liberate" himself from his youthful romanticism. We might ask also why he identified Shelley—and himself—with Shakespeare's Ariel. And why did he feel a need for "liberation?" Long ago Sigmund Freud faced these seemingly unanswerable questions. He was exploring the early life of Leonardo da Vinci. As he put it, in the quaint argot of psychoanalysis, biographers become "fixated on their heroes in a quite special way." He went on:

In many cases they have chosen their hero as the subject of their studies because—for reasons of their own emotional life—they have felt a special affection for him from the very first. They then devote their energies to a task of idealization, aimed at enrolling the great man among the class of their infantile models—at reviving in him, perhaps, the child's idea of his father. To gratify this wish they obliterate the individual features of their subject's physiognomy; they smooth over the traces of his life's struggles with internal and external resistances, and they tolerate in him no vestige of human weakness or imperfection. They thus present us with what is in fact a cold, strange ideal figure, instead of a human being to whom we might feel ourselves distantly related. That they should do this is regrettable, for they thereby sacrifice truth to an illusion, and for the sake of their infantile phantasies abandon the opportunity of penetrating the most fascinating secrets of human nature.

History has many examples of biographers entangled with their subjects—sometimes so entangled that they cannot bring themselves to complete their task; or when they do, they find themselves enmeshed in ambiguities. This is most true of biographers and chroniclers who consort with their subject in the flesh—as Boswell did with Johnson, or Eckermann with Goethe—but it is no less true of those who know their subject exclusively out of an archive. Eckermann did not write a biography; but he was a forerunner of modern "oral history." His conversations with Goethe fascinate. He is admiring, respectful, meticulous and, in a very German way, heavy and grave. There is no question in his mind that Goethe's word is absolute. The great poet is set down with becoming awe, in very human terms. One is certain Eckermann would never be tempted to embroider or invent. His "fixation" demands truth: it becomes a form of loyalty. Boswell too might have written a series of conversations with Johnson; however, he was more ambitious. He felt the need to impose his own structure on his subject, even while pretending to offer a simple story.

Did Boswell select Johnson? Did Johnson pick Boswell? They met and fell into the interesting relation of biographer and subject very much like Goethe and Eckermann. When we ask these questions, we see that the importunities of Boswell and the acceptances of Johnson had deeper roots than we can now know. Johnson certainly knew his mind. He could dismiss fools elegantly. Yet he chose not to dismiss the artfully obvious Boswell. Something attracted him; he was shrewd enough to see that Boswell was half-clown, half-genius. Boswell had a kind of *gauche* sincerity, and a terrifying lack of self-esteem. He was a beguiling man-about-town; his love of gossip, his endless questions, were a challenge to the Doctor—even when Boswell irritated him. Johnson enjoyed scolding Boswell. He amused himself in this friendship; but he could not begin to know how much he pleased Boswell. The younger man had been searching for years for a benign father. His own was a judge who ruled both bench and home like a dictator. Accustomed to depotism. Boswell was on familiar ground with Johnson; his greatest wishes were satisfied. The "mix" ministered to Boswell's low picture of himself; as if he were saying, "yes, I know I am a dog, but Johnson *really* loves me." The lesson we may draw from this is that biographers, whether they deal with the living or the dead, establish some kind of invisible rapport with their subject. The New Biography must ponder this relationship which is usually described in psychiatry as "transference." Biographers have neglected to do so in the past. There must, I take it, be a strong and persistent attraction of some kind to keep the biographer at his work: a boundless curiosity, not unmixed I suppose with a sort of "voyeurism"; a drive to power, common I suppose to most professions; a need for certain forms of omniscience. And there is sometimes that other element—we have all encountered it—the impulse toward accumulation and ingestion of data. This often results in a very cluttered biography—if the work ever gets itself written. We could, I suppose, say much about the biographer's concealed motivations which are converted, when properly channelled, to constructive and artistic ends.

The best, I think, that a biographer can do is to cultivate his awareness and to recognize the constant threat that "involvement" represents to his objectivity. He may then work a little less blindly and ignorantly. By searching for those "fascinating secrets of human nature" of which Freud spoke, by trying to uncover in his subject (and to observe in himself) the "dynamic" and the myth of personality, the biographer may achieve a richer and certainly more sharply focused biography than the biographer who works in the dark. His advantages over other biographers lie, as one psychoanalyst put it, in the understanding of "causal connections, unconscious psychological determinism and the effects of conflicts in family life." To which we might add that he is able, in his speculative process, to recognize the existence of a series of possibilities rather than accept smugly the single answer to any given question projected by himself; and he can try to undermine systematically his own easy rationalizations. In a word, he indulges in fewer rigidities of thought and laxities of feeling, derived from his own fantasies.

I am saying, in effect, that the biographer must try to know himself before he tries to know the life of another. However, self-knowledge, as we well know, is seldom possible. And yet our dilemma is that to write a good biography we must identify ourselves with our subject in some degree. How otherwise reexperience feelings, problems, struggle? We must try to measure the world through the subject's eyes and to penetrate into what those eyes saw. But in becoming this other person for the purpose of biography, the biographer risks everything. This is his overriding anxiety. He must in every sense of the word therefore attempt to be that paradoxical figure which modern psychology has called the "participant-observer." He must be sympathetic yet aloof, involved yet uninvolved. This is the very heart of his struggle.

Lytton Strachey had such dangers in mind when he spoke of the biographer's need to maintain his "own freedom of spirit." The best we can hope for, it would seem, is that the biographer should, as Strachey also said, "lay bare the facts of the case, as he understands them." This is obvious enough and yet it is our best—indeed our sole—reply to the problem of omniscience. A biographer can set forth the data he has gathered only in the light of his own understanding. His understanding is inevitably a "variable," greater or less, depending upon his capacities for interpretation and analysis—and self-observation. The biographer works by the light of his particular resources and intelligence; but he can hardly avoid his own emotions and his empathy: that is, his ability to engage in the adventure of discovering the emotions of his subject in written or verbal utterance and in performance. The greater the biographer's grasp of reality, the more real will his created portrait be. He has absorbed into his operative consciousness a great many documents about another's life. The book that will emerge should be *his* vision, *his* form, *his* picture.

Transference

A̲N ARTIST IN BIOGRAPHY is present in his work in the same way that a painter is present in his portraits. We speak of Boswell as we speak of Titian or Rembrandt. The names of their subjects have sunk into the label under the portraits' frames. The portrait acquires supremacy: the painter looks at a face, a garb, a posture, body movement or repose or some moment of intensity. He achieves this through pictorial skill, color, composition and style. The biographer is signalled in the same way by organization, observation, insight, structure, composition, form and style. As the portrait painter uses pigments and brushes so the biographer uses documents and facts. "Fact and fiction—they are not always easy to distinguish," a character in a novel of Graham Greene remarks—and the entire task of the biographer is a search for the distinction.

Both portrait painters and biographers are permitted few liberties. The demand is for a studied likeness: no prettying up, no retouchings, softenings or hardenings, no pastiche. The artistic statement is most powerful when it is asserted with clarity, lucidity and no vestige of ambiguity. This is what Freud meant in the passage of his *Leonardo* in which he warned biographers not to "smooth over the traces of life's struggles."

Freud was defining the biographer's role as observer-participant. The writer of lives observes a great deal, reads his documents, studies photographs, maps, texts with close attention and acquires mastery over these materials. The participation must be sympathetic rather than empathic. "Transference" must be avoided, that is the danger of a destructive emotional involvement. Virginia Woolf was describing transference when she spoke of "suppression of the self." She meant suppression of the fiction-making self, for if the biographer indulges in fiction the enterprise is doomed. "Transference" is at the core of all biographical writing but biographers resist this conception of their work. They reply they are simply going about their task and finding out what truths they can, so that they may put together a cogent account of their subject's life. What they fail to grasp—and it is extremely diffiult to do so—is that, while they are about their business, their unconscious, or psyche, responds in more ways than they know to their sensory perceptions of their hero or heroine—that subject which has proved so attractive (or sometimes so hateful) that they are prepared to devote some years to their attempt to put it on paper.

The term "transference" is commonly used to describe the singular involvement that occurs in psychiatry between a psychoanalyst and a patient and it is readily applicable to biography. The analyst may be said to be a kind of biographer of the soul; in the therapy he listens with some regularity and with close attention to the patient's inner history: he is not interested so much in the factual *vita* as in dreams, fancies, ideas, moods. One psychological dictionary tells us that "transference" is "the development of an emotional attitude, positive or negative, love or hate, toward the analyst on the part of the patient or subject." Within the frame of these emotions of attachment the analyst begins to see a design, an inexorable logic founded on the patient's earlier conditioning and he uses his therapeutic skills to deal with the patient's emotional colorings and the deep soundings of "affect" that reflect life patternings.

Biographers seek the same information but they usually do not have the living subject available and certainly not the dead; nor is it certain that the subject would be willing to confide except in a manner designed to conceal rather than reveal. Biographers themselves become impatient when the question of their emotional relationship with their subject is raised. They will admit to liking their subject in most cases; they might even confess they have a voyeuristic interest, but they hesitate to discuss what motivated them in their choice, or what promptings they employ in evaluating the life-style of their hero or heroine. What they often struggle against is their own resistance to discovering unpleasant truths, and what their secret selves are up to in shaping the materials. Sooner or later we discover some of the alterations described in Freud's significant warning.

We can best illustrate transference by example. Lytton Strachey's choice of subjects and his treatment of them corresponded to certain deep needs of his psyche. Van Wyck Brooks fashioned one biography after another in his own image. However the example I propose for immediate consideration is André Maurois, their French contemporary, who in his *Aspects of Biography* (1929) describes, without awareness of its implications, an effective "transference" on his own part to his subjects. Maurois, during the first war, worked with the British army and wrote entertainingly about this experience as he acquired mastery of English. He developed an infatuation for Shelley and then swiftly followed his biography of the poet with lives of Disraeli and Byron which won him considerable renown. He was invited by Trinity College, Cambridge (Lytton Strachey's college), to deliver the Clark lectures and chose to talk on aspects of his biographical work following the lead of E. M. Forster who had earlier delivered a series on fiction called *Aspects of the Novel.* Maurois' fourth lecture bore the title "Biography Considered as a Means of Expression."

"Biography," he told his audience, "is a means of expression when the author has chosen his subject in order to respond to a secret need in his own nature." Without knowing it, he here defined transference—for the word "secret" is exactly what Freud was saying when he used the word unconscious. From the moment a biographer responds to "a secret need in his own nature" he is tangled in his emotional relationship with his subject—he is in trouble. Maurois however did not recognize this. What he saw was the delight of his own quasi-amorous feelings. The biography, Maurois said, will be written with "more natural emotion than other kinds of biography, because the feelings and adventures of the hero will be the medium of the biographer's own feelings. To a certain extent it will be autobiography disguised as biography."

We have here a splendid insight arrived at independently of Freud from which however Maurois drew the wrong conclusions. We do not know what assumptions lay behind Maurois' belief that a more "natural" emotion—*une émotion plus naturelle*—is expressed when the biographer develops love for his subject. He was simply forgetting that love is blind; and that this blindness was exactly what leads to retouchings, erasure of wrinkles, and even alterations of character and personality. When a biographer identifies with the subject, the emotions are bound to be more intense, and the result is the blindness that resides in idealization. We can discover that even when a subject is assigned to a biographer or undertaken as a chore for financial considerations, intrusive emotions may enter into the hackneyed job. Identifications and transferences occur whenever some inner chord of feeling is touched. It is precisely the hidden feelings Maurois described as "secret" which can betray, and this is why I said that a biographer must be more sympathetic than empathic—although a certain quantity of aesthetic empathy is inevitable.

Maurois explained that he had been attracted to Shelley because he found so many resemblances between his early romantic feelings and those of the poet. His first impulse was to write a novel about Shelley. This would have enabled him to create a "felt" piece of fiction. His decision to attempt a biography instead suggests that he wanted to hide behind Shelley and make him serve as a mask, to write as he perceived an autobiography disguised as a biography. He did not succeed, for his critics at once found a term for what he was doing—he was writing "romantic lives."

> I was at once irritated by my past youthfulness and indulgent towards it, since I knew that it could not have been otherwise. I longed to expose it, to pillory it, and to explain it at the same time. Well, Shelley had experienced such checks as seemed to me to be somewhat of the same nature as my own . . . Yes, in very truth I felt that to tell the story of his life would be in some measure a deliverance for myself.

The book was a success, but Maurois ultimately found he was not happy with it. Perhaps he recognized that he had falsified Shelley's life. His explanation was that it was spoiled "by an ironic tone which derived from the fact that the irony was aimed at myself. I wanted to kill the romantic in me; in order to do so I scoffed at it in Shelley, but I loved it while I scoffed. Good or bad the book was written with pleasure, even with passion; and now I think you will begin to realize what I mean by biography being considered as a means of expression."

The truth of this declaration is simply that Maurois expressed himself, not Shelley. Let us glance at what occurred in his Disraeli, a larger subject. Shelley died young, Disraeli had a full and completed life. Maurois tells us that the more he read about the British prime minister—the first Jew to attain that high position—he found him a hero "in whom I should have a passionate interest." Of what did that passionate interest consist? Certainly not the fopperies of the young Disraeli, decked out in his gold chains, his fancy waistcoats, his vaulting ambition. Maurois was drawn rather to the Disraeli who discovered the hostility of the world and knew how to deal with his second-rate opponents; who stuck to his principles and displayed a profound humanity in both his private and public relations. Through Disraeli, Maurois could express (though he wasn't a political man) his own democratic conservatism. "Being unable, for very many reasons, to lead a life of political activity myself, I took a passionate pleasure in joining in the struggle by donning the mask of a face that appealed to me."

Again we have "transference." Maurois' use of the words "passion" and "passionate" repeatedly reveals his involvement. There was good reason for his feeling involved, and he suppressed, in the very midst of his public confession, that important bit of information. He did not tell his audience of his deeper ground for iden-tification. André Maurois was the pen name for Émile

Herzog, an Alsation Jew who lived in a France that still echoed to the Dreyfus affair, a country that has always had a strong current of anti-Semitism.

Maurois the young romantic had expressed himself through the young—indeed the never old—Shelley. Maurois the young Jew could express himself through a Disraeli who defied bigotry and achieved the highest kind of success. In his lectures on biography, Maurois did not face his ambivalent feelings. He revealed the familiar unconscious defenses of an outsider, and a member of a maligned race, by uniting himself to Disraeli and his struggle for equality and freedom. In Shelley, he deceived himself by arguing that he was more of an artist than other biographers, since he expressed his emotions through the life-experience of the young English poet. In Disraeli, he deceived himself (and us) by avoiding all allusion to his racial kinship to his hero. He would be more candid in middle life when he wrote his autobiography without using his heroes as disguise. He tells us that (like Disraeli) he had been reared a Protestant and believed he was a Protestant until a school chum told him he was Jewish. Still not believing, he sought out his father who readily confirmed the fact "that we were indeed Jews, but that Pastor Roehrich's Christianity was a beautiful religion too."

Face to face with his thesis about biography "as a means of expression," Maurois finally admitted that he ran the risk "of defacing historical truth." Then self-deception went to work again. Granting that a biographer "has no right to construct a hero according to his own desires and needs," he nevertheless observed that "in rare cases, if the choice is fortunate and well suited to the author's temperament, the biographer may express some of his own feelings without misrepresenting those of the hero." He thus gave himself permission to be "a rare case."

II

Persons with a thorough understanding of the complexities of "transference" would have to say that Maurois' ideal of biography as a form of expression is impossible. The biographer expresses himself or herself not by implanting personal emotions in the subject, but by the "composing" of the biography, by shaping and telling. Maurois was engaged in a full-blown fantasy of himself occupying the shoes of his heroes. Later he invested considerable passion in his life of George Sand, one of the first feminists of modern times. Gender in biography is not in question. Transference can occur in writing of either sex and by members of either sex.

There are so many examples of transference in modern biography that we need not labor the question. But we might glance at the case of Mark Schorer, since he was one of the few biographers who intuitively felt what was happening to him as he struggled to write the life of Sinclair Lewis. His 867-page biography illustrates both the positive and negative identifications. Schorer's account of his experience was described in an essay whose very title suggests his difficulties. He called it "The Burdens of Biography." Addicted biographers would not use the word "burden." It remains one of the rare essays which confesses to mistakes in life-writing and describes the particular problems many biographers avoid.

Schorer begins by telling us that he did not choose to write the life of Lewis. He was invited to do so by a publisher. He wisely adds, "Surely I could have said no." Unlike Maurois, Schorer is willing to see that he was involved in an unconscious process behind his conscious decisions.

I was challenged by what I unconsciously felt to be a strange affinity, an affinity perhaps only demonstrated by the fact that my literary tastes, as they matured, had moved about as far away from his [Lewis's] as is possible. There was, of course, the obvious affinity of our beginnings—the same kind of raw small Midwestern towns, probably much the same kind of inept and unsuccessful boys in that particular man's world. But I discovered many more, and many that were more subtle ... all the careless writing, all the ill-conceived ambitions, all the bad manners, all the irrational fits of temper, all the excesses of conduct, all the immature lifelong frivolities and regrettable follies. That is a little of it. There is much more.

Like Maurois, the American biographer indulges in self-criticism. At the same time we are shown the extent to which Schorer became enmeshed in his subject, more profoundly than he knew. It is to his credit that he discerned this, for he speaks of his "symbiotic relationship" with Lewis, or what another critic called his "nine year's captivity with him." Schorer concludes:

My long conversation with Sinclair Lewis ... taught me a good deal. As I learned about him with all his stubborn deficiency in self-knowledge, I believe that I gained in self-knowledge. I am not a better man, certainly, for having written his life, but I think I am a wiser one. And I can only hope that my gratitude to him for that will lighten a little the onus of the life with which I have burdened him.

What were the consequences of Schorer's transference? He was not always sure what to use and what to discard. He had no firm grip, no sense of his own authority, with the result that he floundered. He tended to reiterate certain life patterns as the critics immediately noticed. Instead of describing an archetypal Lewis drunk, he led his readers through the vicissitudes of repeated drinking bouts. This represented a failure to see the proportions of the life he was writing. He began by feeling that he and Lewis had much in common: but then he grew weary of Lewis and the transference shifted from positive to negative. That was why he used the word "burden" to describe his job of work—a job that in other circumstances could be a creative challenge. There are some fine passages of biographical writing in this heavy book. But the confusion in his psyche undermined his project and he was ultimately swamped by his too-abundant materials.

III

There is another recent instance of this kind of difficulty. As is well known, Lawrance Thompson was appointed by Robert Frost to be his Boswell. It took very little time for Thompson to become deeply involved with the poet—his relationship moved from casual acquaintance to friendship, from friendship to familiarity, from familiarity to dislike and from dislike to animosity. In Thompson's eyes Frost became a demanding authority. The poet called on his Boswell to amuse him and grace his lonely hours. He would go to Florida for a holiday and telephone Thompson to come down and play cards and keep him entertained. By the time Frost died, Thompson was ready to arraign his subject as arrogant, jealous, resentful, sulky, vindictive and addicted to tempers and rages. Readers of Thompson's biography, which was never fully completed, remember that what emerged was a merciless portrayal of Frost's egotism and its devastating effect on those close to him. How accurate this was, we are not in a position to say: it would have to be examined and reevaluated by some new and more objective biographer. We do know that Robert Frost foresaw some of Thompson's ambivalences. In his letters to Thompson he shows for example a certain concern that he would be made out to be more religious than he ever was—in conformity with Thompson's own religious emotions. "I grow curious about my soul," he teased his Boswell, "out of sympathy for you in your quest for it." Frost's concern in this instance was well founded. Thompson did dismiss certain of his blasphemies, saying that Frost never rejected his faith for very long. He compared him in one instance with Job—and this in the face of Frost's religious skepticism.

Few biographers can escape forms of transference, least of all the "idealization" transference exemplified in Maurois' early works. But deeper forms may be seen, those in which the entire biographical pursuit of certain writers became a drive to complete themselves in their works. Let us look at what happened to Lytton Strachey.

LYTTON STRACHEY

DID LYTTON STRACHEY maintain his "freedom of spirit" in the salient short biographies which he compounded with consistent irony and an aphoristic style?—his four essays in *Eminent Victorians,* his distilled portrait of Queen Victoria, his attempt to read himself into an older England, in *Elizabeth and Essex?* One feels, certainly, that in the latter work he labored as one trapped by his own methods, and by his own subject. What was his subject? What were his methods? His subject was the British establishment, "the mingling contradictions of the English spirit"—Victorian hypocrisy, the combination of British strength and creativity, which made England and its empire into an instrument of power, privilege and piety, neurosis and conquest, presided over at two poles of history by Elizabeth, and a ruthless aristocracy, and Victoria and middle-class domesticity. This was a great edifice built upon centuries of profound belief and self-confidence, expediency and action, and incredible pride; also ultimately philistine smugness and an overweening moral righteousness: world-shaking events and little men quoting their Bible to assuage fear and melancholy and to fortify themselves against their awareness of the Abyss. Cardinal Manning and his essentially ruthless career; Thomas Arnold and his

Christian education—the Bible and respectability; Gordon, the Christian general, who committed folly in the belief that he was serving God and country, and Florence Nightingale, with her soft legend of "The Lady of the Lamp," who was as hard as nails and knew how to defy and conquer. These were some of Strachey's characters. His work, in its larger sense, pits strong queenly women against puny men, and endows the women with masculine strength, feminine endurance and feminine-masculine action. Lytton Strachey's works show in striking fashion the biographer's ability to rise above his own struggles and project into history fabled versions of his personal drama. To that extent, Strachey's work was determined (as with all artists) in his own psyche. This is not to say that he was aware of what was happening. It is a part of man's endowment to live in ignorance of what his genes are plotting and to act in seeming freedom in spite of the predeterminations of history, environment and the residual habits of early years. Strachey's freedom resided in the way in which an artist *fulfills* the promptings of personal fairies and demons. The dictates are answered; the predetermined choices appear to us as unexpected accidents of the imagination. Strachey's fable or life-image (and we have Holroyd's bulging volumes to provide abundant evidence) was a dramatization of his own complex relation to the presiding Queen of Lancaster Gate, Lady Strachey, his mother, a power, an inflexible, determined, unassailable woman, capable of action like Florence Nightingale, smothered in domesticity, possessing a houseful of children, like Victoria, and able to rule like Elizabeth. In dealing with these women of power, Lytton Strachey could study the drama of his own relation to his queen-mother, who had visibly and invisibly guided his life and against whose establishment he had rebelled. He learned to cope with his own manipulative and assertive homosexuality by becoming the very queens of his stories. In his fertile imagination he could be the mother of his numerous boys—and at the same time their lover. In his androgynous role, wearing the masks of the queenly woman, he became at times a too-terrifying mother of the young he pursued and embraced. They often fled from his suffocating embraces—as witness Duncan Grant's turning from him to the more rational and detached figure of J.M. Keynes. But in these high romantic and dramatic episodes, Strachey could feel himself as supreme and as powerful as the queens had been, and with this he could—in his work—use his prickly nature, his awareness of ironies, his sense of his own ambiguity, to demonstrate in modern biography what Freud had already demonstrated in his case histories: that a subject, a case, a human being, is not as consistent, logical, plain and straightforward as biographers have long believed. Even God's created children of the Old Testament were never all of a piece. They were irrational, inexplicable, mysterious, self-contradicting, to be rendered with all their ambivalences, hence true subjects for ironies of the most delicate kind. Irony being the play of invisible or felt opposites, it proved the perfect instrument for portraying ambivalence in greatness. Strachey, in describing Manning's devious use of power, could use as experience his own manipulative skill; he could also be Florence Nightingale, upsetting the inertia of Whitehall and making herself the mother of an entire army of men: delightful thought to a homoerotic like Strachey. On the other hand, when he was not identifying with his queen-women, Strachey could portray seemingly ridiculous male figures—General Gordon, or Arnold (the one commander of men, the other educator of boys)—lampooning in these figures his talented father, methodical, mild, soft, art-and-nature loving General Strachey, who in his old age sat in an armchair reading novels, oblivious of the life of his numerous progeny around him.

What were Strachey's methods? He told us in his characteristic way that the modern biographer faced with vast documentation has to "attack his subject in unexpected places"; to "shoot a sudden revealing searchlight into obscure recesses, hitherto undivined"; "to illustrate rather than explain." And then, in his rhetoric, we are aware of his brevity, his splendid art of summary—the truly admirable traits of his work—his use of the telling phrase, a kind of sharpness in drawing that explained itself in the very process of delineation. Less admirable, but still having a certain validity, was his tendency to create pastiche. He often placed on the page words of his subjects without direct quotation. This was not an act of plagiarism; it was a direct attempt to conduct his readers into his characters rather than have them look at them from the outside. Such a mosaic insinuates to the reader that he is sharing the actual thoughts of the personage. In doing this. Strachey practised at moments biographical fiction; he crossed that forbidden frontier only to dart back into the realm of document and fact. Who can claim to record the helter-skelter of thought and feeling in a human being—at any time? The inner world is seen always in reflection in a diary, in letters; in utterance, in written record; it is never tape-recorded for us in the past. As a method of evoking motives and attitudes, of giving us the flavor and the spirit—the perfumes of thought—Strachey's method had extraordinary effect; but it had a kind of sleight-of-hand, a magician's cunning trickery. Thus when he wrote out the backgrounds of Queen Victoria's reign, gathering moments of her life into a peroration, as she lay dying, as if these constituted her actual stream of consciousness, Strachey achieved nostalgic beauty, the very elegiac tone that he had lamented in biography. But he was breaching the wall of fact. The reader had an arbitrary delight. Was he reading Victoria's thoughts or Strachey's? In a passage on Newman, in his essay on Cardinal Manning, we can observe the ways in which Strachey makes us party to Newman's thoughts—a kind of fantasy created by the biographical narrator:

> Newman was now an old man—he was sixty-three years of age. What had he to look forward to? A few last years of insignificance and silence. What had he to look back upon? A long chronicle of wasted efforts, disappointed hopes, neglected possibilities, unappreciated powers. And now all his labours had ended by his being accused at Rome of a lack of orthodoxy.

The passage is typical of Strachey's art of summary. But it is made to read as if Newman himself were indulging in personal stock-taking and self-disparagement. There may be such a passage somewhere in Newman's writings. One does not know, however, for Strachey never supplied footnotes. He was seeking to write a kind of work that would require no gloss. Still the reader questions whether so devout a personality would indulge in so much self-doubt without mitigating thoughts about the ways of God and God's will. That use of the interrogative, What had he to look forward to? What had he to look back upon? was Strachey's. Yet it sounded as if the questions were being asked by Newman. Newman as a good Christian looked forward to his union with the divine spirit: to the beneficence of death. The method is ingenious. It has its obvious dangers.

... in Manning's soul ... that voice was never silent. Whatever else he was, he was not unscrupulous. Rather, his scruples deepened with his desires; and he could satisfy his most exorbitant ambitions in a profundity of self-abasement. And so now he vowed to Heaven that he would *seek* nothing—no, not by lifting of a finger or the speaking of a word. But if something came to him—? He had vowed not to seek; he had not vowed not to take. Might it not be his plain duty to take? Might it not be the will of God?

Again we wonder whether a diary is being paraphrased: and the indirect style here acquires a hidden dimension. The lay reader finds it convincing; but the practising biographer, the critic, the scholar, is conscious of subterfuge and licence. Such are the intimate perils of Stracheyesque biography. The author gives us, in a bibliography, the volumes he read and used. The question is, *how* have they been used?

A whole generation of biographers—Guedalla in England, Maurois in France. Van Wyck Brooks in America—was seduced by Strachey's devices and aphoristic glibness; he breathed a superb omniscience, and then he was always witty, always amusing, always seeking the ways of art. It was very well to "attack" one's subject "in unexpected places"; to "shoot" his light into recesses. But what kind of attack? What kind of shooting? The theory is sound even if the words are aggressive. Given voluminous archives, the high example could be sought amid clutter; Strachey's little bucket could be lowered into the Victorian lake to bring up specimens: the characteristic episode, the illuminating gesture. But the phrase was quicker than the eye. And the phrase could kill.

Strachey recognized in his work that man is less logical than biographers make him out to be. Biographers of the past used to iron out inconsistencies. They imposed their own systematic minds upon material that reflected the inexplicable and the mysterious, the irrationality of human character. What Strachey recognized was that irony was the best tool for portraying conflict, ambiguity, ambivalence. The play of subterranean opposites sufficed to make his figures fallible and fallibly luminous.

Strachey illustrates, in a precise way, the manner in which a biographer, choosing his subject, tends to be chosen by it. The underlying animus in all that Strachey wrote reflects his own demonic malaise. His genius for character was strong; his personal ambitions were quite as strong. There were moments when he could be as unprincipled in his art as some of his characters were in life. If he needed a jewel around the neck of Queen Elizabeth, he simply put it there—an artist adding a spot of colour to a portrait. But for all his inventions and sculpturing of his materials, he caught and gave us humans in the grip of their compulsions and passions, and showed how each fulfilled, or failed to fulfill, his destiny. The lesson of Strachey for the New Biography is a valuable lesson, both in its faults and virtues. What is needed fairly obviously is some middle road between his excesses of invention, his addiction to plausible yet often misleading pastiche, his deceptive rhetorical devices and the more sober monotony of fact-finding, and fact-compiling. For all his mischievous errors we can salute him as an eccentric father of modern biography. He overthrew the obsolete model, James Boswell.

VAN WYCK BROOKS

LYTTON STRACHEY had one important American disciple, a devoted emulator of his rhetorical and biographical innovations. The influence has not been recognized, yet it is unmistakeable. His disciple was Van Wyck Brooks, who caught the attention of his generation by his espousal of "American studies" and his insistence upon America's "useable" past. What he meant by this is not altogether clear. "Useable"—to whom, and for what? Van Wyck Brooks's use of the past was highly personal, most often a choice, not wholly conscious, of whatever lent itself to the problems that challenged *his* mind. He was a deeply troubled "man of letters." His very countenance—the candid eyes, the big bushy moustache, the sad world-searching manner—were in accord with his use of history in a seemingly impersonal way—but for personal ends. Brooks was on the whole a better prose writer than Strachey. His prose was liquid, and it had a singular grace lacking in his English contemporary's more aphoristic and astringent manner. Strachey was light-handed and flexible in his mockeries. Brooks never mocked. He was solemn and imitative; he revelled in "character"; he liked idiosyncrasy; and although he was regarded as a "critic" he made no attempt to draw sharp critical lines. He lacked Strachey's intellectual and critical power. He also lacked self-assurance and Strachey's stance of authority. A man of tender poetic and artistic feeling, Brooks somehow had not allowed himself to be poet or painter. His intellectual aspirations led him into critical-historical writing of a mindless sort: "mindless" in that he bent his materials always to prove a thesis; he advocated social reform that reflected stasis and the rigidities of the past. He wished to make the past "useable"—to prove something: but it was not at all the kind of "proving" that Strachey indulged in. Strachey's aim was to show the self-righteousness and pomposity of the Victorians, to treat their "eminence" in a light ironic way that ended by questioning it. His work moreover was informed by the new psychology. His brother, James Strachey, was a psychoanalyst and ultimately the translator into English of Freud's entire work. Psychoanalysis in its earliest forms was in the air: and Strachey grasped certain of Freud's fundamental tenets—those most useful to biography: man's gift for altering experience in his imagination and therefore altering his concept of himself, in a word, the forms of human self-delusion. As Cardinal Manning told himself indirectly that his ambitions were sanctioned by God, so Strachey found sanction for his judgment of figures in the past in the arrogance and strength of his own intellect, in the logic of his wit, the vigor and sharpness of his perceptions. He was honest to the extent that he announced he was laying bare his facts as he understood them. But "understanding" is as subjective as "useable"—both being all too often the result of wishful thinking. Freud nevertheless helped Strachey to know the meaning of ambivalence.

Van Wyck Brooks never learned this lesson, although he read Freud. His unhappiness drove him always to things of the past. The present was too painful. He possessed the kind of mind that did not allow him to depart from fixed ideas. How these ideas became fixed, and the influence they had on his biographical writing, can be grasped only by examining the struggles of his earlier years. He was the child of a strong society woman, an American "queen," rooted in America's materialism. She believed that men belonged in the business world (doubtless the better to provide affluence for their wives); and she imparted to her two sons a destructive concept of masculinity. Business was masculine; the arts were feminine. This was reinforced by their vision of a sensitive father, who had lived abroad and taken on many European ways, but who was tethered against his better judgment to Wall Street. The peculiar "logic" of Brooks's life-myth resolved itself into a masculine-feminine "double bind." In the arithmetic of his psyche, to be a man like his father meant being a slave to business; on the other hand to embrace art, as his mother had done in her superficial socialite way, meant a denial of manhood. Brooks lived constantly in this terrible state of conflict; and in self-defence, with more emotion than reason, he set out to show that art, too, is robust and manly. That this meant a dismissal of some of the best qualities in art did not occur to Brooks; however, it explains his inability during his entire life to understand the most important writers of our time. His "either-or" mind could not acquiesce in the blessings of androgyny. His life was a quest—and a questioning—of the male-female bondage in which he found himself. In putting his case in this fashion I am not suggesting that he was consciously aware of his trouble. It is implicit however in all that he wrote.

His first book, *The Wine of Puritans,* exalted Europe over America; and he thought of himself as defying his mother in writing it. In all that he wrote he expressed his eternal love-hate. He loved Europe. Then he felt ashamed of this love. He disliked America. This gave him strong feelings of guilt. He turned around and exalted America. Each step was an aggression against father-or-mother, country-or-society, because he had no neutral ground in his make-up. There was no such thing as having *both* America and Europe; no such thing as being both male and female; one had always to choose. His elder brother chose business—but ultimately resolved his conflict by jumping in front of a train. Brooks, after a long struggle—he called it his "season in hell"—attempted suicide several times. He rescued himself by writing *The Flowering of New England*. In that flowering he was born anew.

Brooks's difficulties in self-acceptance and the stratifications of his inner world were expressed in all that he wrote. "It becomes our responsibility as a composite people to unite the virtues of all races," he said when he was young, and "this building up of ideal manhood is the Mission of American Art." "Ideal manhood" could allow itself love of beauty, culture, civilization. "Harmonized, softened, idealized" such manhood could combine the ruggedness of a Lincoln with the softness of a Raphael—"eloquent beauty and sturdy Manhood." And then "we have a mighty slough of commercialism that only art can reconcile with the Ideal." Brooks's search for the "Ideal" was a search for his own "ideal Manhood." In three small books written between 1913 and 1915, he worked hard to tell himself how he would arrive at this blessed state. He treated three "failed" writers in Europe, who like himself wandered into compromises—Amiel, Sénancour and Maurice de Guérin. He called the first book *The Malady of the Ideal;* the three writers failed of fulfillment he said because they sought an ideal and expended their art in letter-writing or keeping diaries (as Brooks expended his poetry in trying to be a literary critic): they had not found the requisite alternatives. Each of these figures became thus a mirror for Brooks's own troubled countenance. The possibility that their lives took the only form that they could find was not acceptable to Brooks. Things should have been otherwise. His second volume dealt with John Addington Symonds, the historian and biographer who, as we now know, was a crusading homosexual. In the Victorian world Symonds had to conceal the one subject at the centre of his emotions and passions behind a love of the Greeks, poetry and the voluptuous in Italian art. Brooks latched on to this illustrative figure; since he had to conceal his love of art in favour of a masculinity in American life distasteful to him, he read with ease in Symonds this writer's failure to express what he really wanted to say. Symonds was forced to conceal his real masculine nature; he could not accept the feminine. At least in his private life, he found the pleasures of love between man and man which Brooks's puritanism and conflict denied him. Indeed Brooks looked away from the evidence of Symonds's eager homoeroticism. The solution? The American found it in his third book, a long essay on H. G. Wells. Wells satisfied the prophet in Brooks, the reformer, the critic, the preacher, the journalist, the man who wanted to change any social order that exalted materialism at the expense of art. Wells, said Brooks, was an artist "disturbed by the absence of the right composition in human beings." He dealt in the "real." We may wonder today that Brooks saw as "real" a writer whose greatest success lay in what we now disguise as "futurism"—the writing of utopias and science

[87

fiction. In fact Wells too was looking for an "ideal." He thought that socialism might be the answer. He worked always (in his own imagination) on "the shape of things to come."

Having written this trilogy—three stages in his quest for a masculine-feminine peace—Van Wyck Brooks proceeded to write a second trilogy. Now he chose three American "cases." He wrote "the ordeal" of Mark Twain, the "pilgrimage" of Henry James and finally settled on a rather strange American parallel to H. G. Wells— Ralph Waldo Emerson. During the writing of these books, Brooks was in and out of sanitoriums; he had terrible depressions; his life continually crumbled. What he tried to show was that Mark Twain and Henry James had been "failures." In Emerson, however, he had an American model that represented success. Brooks's series of "Eminent Americans" seemed to endow them with ordeals and pilgrimages which belonged to himself. He asserted that materialistic America had thwarted the strong genius of the Mississippi in Clemens. Instead of accepting the life-dilemma of Mark Twain, its successes and failures and the ways in which that vigorous, troubled, sympathetic man dealt with his problems, Van Wyck Brooks constructed a particular experience. Mark Twain had been forced to treat his art as if it were a business enterprise. He was a failure because of his "moral surrender." He had placed his genius at the service of "the efficiency of the business regime." As a result, the poet in Mark Twain "withered into the cynic" who could talk only of "the damned human race."

In Henry James, Brooks collided with a submerged iceberg. James had embraced Europe and remained abroad in happy exile. His art had become increasingly complex; he had had disappointing flirtations with the theatre. He was a reasonable bachelor who refused to be a reformer. Brooks wrote of James as if he were composing a scrapbook of related quotations—and in emulation of Strachey he did not tell his readers when he was quoting and when the observations were his own. In a prefatory note he explained that he was resorting to this expediency because he knew of "no other means of conveying with strict accuracy at moments what he conceives to have been James's thoughts and feelings." This was a strange rationalization: there has never been a biographer who could reproduce the inner world of his subject; the best he can do is to describe it. Brooks's appropriation of passages from James's fiction and criticism—wholly out of context—resulted in a collage; he created a Henry James who always wore the mask of Van Wyck Brooks. And he painted a portrait of James's decline as an artist. In the eyes of Brooks, James too was a "failure" like Mark Twain. In his case he had torn up his roots by leaving America; his work therefore was rootless. Brooks felt that exile produced the vague "miasmic" of James's final novels in which James he said wandered like a lost soul between two worlds. That the evidence was all against him did not trouble Brooks until much later, when he admitted that the *Pilgrimage of Henry James* taught him "the division within myself." It did not, however, eradicate that division.

In these two biographies Brooks used powerful creative figures in American letters as if he had been hypnotized by them; he felt out the core of depression in Twain and James, and then read their personal dilemmas as if they were his own. Edmund Wilson was among the first to reprimand him for what he had done. Brooks, Wilson wrote, had undertaken to be a critic with "intense zeal at the service of intense resentment." He said that

Brooks wanted to protest against the spiritual poverty of America, in its discouragement of the creative artist. In preaching this doctrine, said Wilson, Brooks was attacking the victims along with the American conditions from which they had suffered. Wilson had the feeling that Brooks was hounding down "poor old James" as he had hounded down "poor old Mark Twain."

Brooks saw Emerson as a whole man, a "male" consciousness, the American model he had sought. In his *Life of Emerson* Brooks conveniently overlooked Emerson's ordeals and pilgrimages, his years of crisis; Emerson too had had a large amount of suffering before he became an oracle in Concord's apple orchards. In Emerson, Brooks saw a writer who had fulfilled himself, to be sure not in the imaginative art forms which said little to the sage, but as a writer of pithy epigrammatic essay-sermons. From his small bit of American territory Emerson contemplated the universe. Through Emerson, Brooks could make his own deeper philistinism and conservatism acceptable; he could justify his compromises and conceal his shame and guilt. He turned the picturesque provincialism of Concord to happy account. Out of this view he wrote his five volumes of America's literary "makers and finders," seeing not the achievement of American writers so much as their homely aspects, the homelier the better. He found a deep kinship with Howells, with Aldrich, with the worthies of the *Atlantic*—in a word, with the bourgeois world of Boston and Concord. He could exalt Thoreau and accept Whitman—in the way that he had closed his eyes to Symonds. In the years of comparative serenity that followed, he looked back at his Mark Twain as his "inferno." James had been his "purgatorio"; he had dreams during one of his breakdowns of James looking at him with his "great menacing luminous eyes." Emerson however was his "paradiso." In this way he made the lives of others minister to his own well-being. His is one of the most unusual case-histories of distortion of the biographical subject.

How exactly did he imitate Strachey? A striking example of the way in which he used one Stracheyean "trick" can be given:

> *Strachey in Manning's thoughts:* "All these things were obvious, and yet—and yet—. Might not the formal declaration etc."
>
> *Brooks in the thoughts of Henry James, Senior:* "It was all possible ... and yet, and yet ... He could not surrender the beloved vision etc."

Where Strachey, however, produced thoughts that remained "in character," Brooks produced thoughts by the same methods (disregard of quotation and context) which altered character.

Strachey accepted himself as homosexual, and had no difficulty in writing about strong women and weak men. Brooks could not accept the most benign side of himself which might have been homosexual. His strong mother had laid down the inflexible lines of his world. He seems to have been fixed in them as in a strait jacket. Hence, while Strachey saw the reality of his subjects but coloured them through the lens of his often hostile feelings towards them, Brooks always saw his subjects *as they should have been,* if they had lived in a Brooksian world. His real quest was to remake himself. His process was the peculiar one we have described—the biographer putting on illusory masks of others, after altering the masks to correspond to his own illusions.

And so we see that the biographer, first on a subliminal level and later more consciously is involved at every stage of his task in a game of "me" and "not me." The success of the biography depends on the degree to which a biographer disengages himself from his alter ego—his subject. The modern biographer has to seek the seemingly contradictory ways of detachment, participation, observation in the interest of truth. We can affirm that the poet is his poem, the novelist his novel. By the same token the biographer is always his biography—*and not his subject*. When the biographer has learned this lesson, he can distance himself, question himself, question his materials, above all question his preferences. These can constitute personal wishes rather than the impersonal facts of the case. Justice likes to think of itself as blind, and therefore impartial; biography cannot afford to be blind—but its goal is always a proper impartiality, a need to allow the subject its life—as it was lived—not as the biographer wishes it to have been lived.

Archives

BIOGRAPHY, like history, is the organization of human memory. Assembled and hoarded papers are bits and pieces of this memory. Filing cabinets and memory machines are a part of its technology. The Elizabethans were far too active discovering an expanding world to bother with records. They lived in the present—too much so to muse on the past or to file their papers. Indeed they had precious little paper, the use of which may be said to have begun (though introduced in the fourteenth century) when Sir John Spilman, a goldsmith to Queen Elizabeth, built a paper mill at Dartford just about the time the British were defeating the Spanish Armada. One regrets they did not use more, so that biographers would not have to scrape and piece together the few details we possess of Shakespeare's life.

I

The archive, and in particular the personal archive, belongs to modern times. There are famous isolated collections of papers in the distant past. These were happy accidents, examples of system or frugality which occurred by chance in private households. It is we who have had to shore up, as best we can, the relics of the less self-conscious centuries; and these being fragmentary and fortuitous, what we know may indeed be of less importance than what we might have otherwise known.

At one moment we work in a past where there is a broken column, a piece of mosaic, a headless torso, then we cross a historical boundary and we are in possession of clothes, furniture, bills, relics, deeds, letters, the very houses themselves, and portraits—fragments of a more approachable, a more visitable past. Yet even this material does not bring us to our age of the archive. How recent our archive-sense is may be judged by the fact that although there was a congress of archivists in the United States in 1909, the Society of American Archivists was not founded until 1936. The American National Archive was established two years earlier, in 1934. The Historical Records Survey, stimulated by Rooseveltian measures to cope with the depression, was conducted between 1936 and 1943. The Federal Records Act is of 1950.

If this seems very late in the day, it is not much later than what happened in Europe, given the long reach of European history. It took the French Revolution to establish France's national archive. There were great collections of papers in France of an earlier time, and men like Saint-Simon to offer us a multitude of pictures of a given reign. But the Archives Nationales is of 1789 and the Archives Départementales date from 1796. By this, Republican France recognized that the state had a responsibility for the national memory. The Reichsarchiv at Potsdam, to take another example, dates only from 1919. Public access to archives followed as a matter of course. We recognize therefore that the modern archive-process has gone hand in hand with the democratic process and with the growth of national establishments.

Yet even the establishment of national archives does not begin to suggest the extent to which we have become hoarders of the relics of our immediate past. We now build entire libraries to house the papers of our presidents; and thanks to the existence of carbon paper and photocopying we have in these libraries copies of letters, millions of them, which in other eras would be dispersed all over the world and in the possession only of the recipients. And I speak of even a later moment, when we possess not only the papers of the president but tape recordings of his speeches, kinescopes, movies—for these, too, are documents—and all the records of public relations by which what we call the presidential "image" is created and recreated. And that is not all.

There are also the archives and the memories of those who served the president. An entire cabinet, a staff, the secretaries who typed the letters, the assistants, the technicians—all are watching this man, and many are taking notes. Is there any question of his awareness that notes are being taken? He is the man who, as never before—more than the fabled kings of old—stands constantly before the mirror of history and of time. The public, we know, is encouraged to believe that Hyde Park—or the Kennedy Library—contain everything related to these presidencies. It is nourished on the thought of completeness, and television biographies revive films and the remembered voice, so that the spectators are made to feel that there is nothing an archive (or the "morgue" of a magazine or newspaper) cannot yield. Nevertheless important gaps remain. For no man in the public eye can pretend he doesn't know that he must talk in private. There may be greater showers of paper than ever—but where are the telephone calls of yesteryear—and telephone calls on private lines? Some of course are in the FBI files. But others have achieved nonexistence. The intimate personal conferences—the smoke-filled rooms of tradition—where no minutes are kept and everyone has a different version when the smoke clears—these contain hidden history—*l'envers de l'histoire contemporaine,* as Balzac said. Our press secretaries, moreover, have cultivated the art of making everything seem public even while the truth remains private. Does history then become something else—something premeditated, planned, staged, ghostwritten? Only something like an assassin's bullet, it would seem, brings into play spontaneities in human events, and certain mysteries return to our midst.

I am not aware that anyone has inquired whether presidential libraries are necessary to the intellectual life of the republic, in the quantity in which we seem to be accumulating them. Franklin D. Roosevelt's library at Hyde Park was a logical outcome of his presidential longevity. He was in office for a period that could truly be described as an "era," and his personal archive, in addition to the public archive, assumed considerable proportions: it encompassed the depression of the 1930s, and the second war. One could claim without argument the usefulness to historians and biographers of keeping FDR's papers in one place, and in a place consonant with the memories of his family and his family history. But what of the presidents who have followed? Surely a "normal" term of office does not require a mausoleum-library? And yet we seem to be accepting such libraries as routine. Failing monuments in Washington, reserved for transcendant figures, documentary repositories are created for some presidents perhaps in the hope of enlarging their historical niche. These may complicate rather than simplify research, even though one might be tempted to say, in general, that the more libraries we can have—

in any nation—the better. The presidential libraries also seem to house mementos and materials relevant to museums. Or to put it another way, what do these libraries harbor that cannot be contained within the normal facilities provided by our national institutions? The presidential libraries imply—to the public at least—that the lives of the holders of the highest office are completely documented in these show-buildings. But they are, in reality, branch establishments of the National Archive. The full history of, say, the Truman presidency, is not in his library in Missouri, nor can the history of the abbreviated Kennedy presidency be contained in the Cambridge memorial building. The State Department archives still have to be consulted; the Pentagon at some time will have to declassify some of its materials for future historians and researchers, and foreign libraries will continue to have materials inevitably not found on American soil.

These libraries are therefore of limited use, often disguised museums rather than research centers, and they belong to the artificial archive-making of public relations. Half a million photographs of Lyndon B. Johnson may be viewed in Austin, Texas. As one newspaper remarked with a grin, "scholars doubt that there would have been room for 500,000 photographs in the Great Pyramid at Giza." The library offers "instant" forms of history as well. There is close-circuit television showing nonstop highlights of Johnson's career. There are thirty-one million Johnson documents available to any historian making his way into the mausoleum. Much of this material is of questionable importance; a goodly amount of it can be characterized as wastepaper basket. But how extricate from such massive clutter the necessary and the useful?

II

Has the legend-making and the myth-making of our time changed the essential work of the biographer? I think it has simply increased his physical labor. There are more papers to push around, and a thick wall of words called "public relations" to be penetrated. Order must be brought; a coherent story needs to be told, meanings interpreted and explained. However overwhelming, the archives must be mastered or they will smother the researchers.

From the moment we envisage biography as an art, we must see that the compendium-biography is the marble, roughhewn, delivered from the quarry. The sculptor's work remains to be done. If a biography of Franklin D. Roosevelt were written on the scale of Nicolay and Hay's life of Lincoln, we would probably require a hundred volumes; and how many would be needed, on the same scale, to tell the life of Churchill? The compendium-biography is in reality a gathering-in of documents, texts, entire letters, editorials, the kind of materials that belong under glass in an exhibition. No one will deny the place of the omnium-gatherum life; we must nevertheless recognize it for what it is.

Richard Ellmann once argued that "biographies should be long," but one could not tell whether he was being ironic or Victorian. A biography should find its own length; and the length is prescribed by the dimensions of the subject, perspective, a sense of relevance. It should never be a way of stuffing in all the little facts on the theory that every surviving scrap, every tiny button, has importance. Facts have importance only in a chain of evidence.

In describing the monumentality of modern archives

I am not for one moment deprecating their importance or value. How can literary scholars and historians not be grateful for Harvard's gathering in of the personal archives of Concord—Emerson, Thoreau, the Alcotts, Hawthorne, Melville and so many others; their great James collection and the papers of so many Cambridge and Boston worthies? To mention these is but to scrape the surface. Yale's collection of modern writers, the treasures of Texas, the judicious gathering-in of the Berg Collection in the New York Public Library, C. Waller Barrett's Americana in Virginia—and I speak here only of the eastern seabord; westward we find the Lilly Library in Indiana—but I skip and jump, and I do not forget Robert Taylor's highly selective holdings at Princeton. To enumerate these, is to pass over many others and research scholars know where to go and where to find such holdings as are scrutinized in despair by those who work in the lean centuries and have to rely on the oral tradition. Yet even this more discreet and informed archive-making, as distinct from the Library of Congress where veritable cartloads are deposited, has entered a new and dramatic phase. There came a moment when the libraries were not content to wait until writers were dead and the papers in the hands of their executors. The libraries began to approach the living. They provided new sources of income and urged writers to keep their correspondence, the various drafts of their work and their scribbles and doodles which sometimes fill the margins of their pages. A kind of self-consciousness crept into the process: the autograph market became the coordinate of the royalty statement; and if authors accepted the proposals that papers pass from their desks into the inviolable boxes and filing cabinets to be kept in acid-free folders, the papers yielded the benefits of tax deduc-

tion (although subsequent legislation blocked this loop-
hole and deprived libraries of valuable sources of modern
cultural material). Still there are poets who have found
comfort not through publication of their poems but
through the sale of their manuscripts.

The state was for a while the double benefactor and
patron of the library of deposit and of the depositor. We
discover a parallel between the president, with his multi-
authored speech and the multiplied recording media,
and the private author who suddenly faces serious
inducements to create archives larger than were intended
by life and the career of art. Readers of Lawrance
Thompson's anthology of Robert Frost's letters must have
been struck by Frost's easy cynicism in such matters.
Fame had come; he knew that his signature on a book,
and the airy trifles and jokes he could scribble in his own
hand, were commercial objects. He played with these
and created them with a kind of childlike glee. If the
world wanted some of the inconsequential relics of a
poet, why, let it have them, especially if his own pocket
could thereby be the more comfortably lined.

I have friends whose archives are now in certain
American libraries, handsomely paid for. When I write
to them I feel literary history breathing down my neck.
I choose my words, I repress certain emotions, I tend to
be secretive. Self-consciousness puts its hand upon mine.
I find myself admonishing correspondents not to pho-
tocopy and circulate what I have written. I no longer
can be privately angry or libellous. I once wrote an angry
letter which was promptly copied and sent to the very
person who should not have been exposed to my anger.
Privacy is at an end.

In the old days, houses were blessed with fireplaces and much paper was automatically consigned to flames. Now, with the advent of modern heating, a great convenience to authors has been removed. The age of the archive, with a pecuniary motivation that is irresistible and beneficient, tells the poet and man of letters that there is no use for the wastepaper basket. Every chance scribble belongs to posterity. All the proofs and rewrites, every last tedious exchange with a publisher or an editor, even of relative value. Splendid indeed for graduate students when the stuff is assembled in one place. It is less than splendid—it is formidable and frightening—when the biographer must confront trivia. For this archive-making creates curious situations in which spontaneity flies up the chimney—or since that image is obsolete, out of the wastepaper basket. Many research library purchases are justified by the needs for graduate study and doctoral dissertations. And it is true that research is helped when everything is available in one place. But are we not making life too easy for the young? Shouldn't they be required to have the fun of research as well as the abundance—the sleuthing in attics, the hunt in hole-in-wall places, the trips to past scenes of literary activity? And how qualified is the novice to handle the subtleties of epistolary art? Exposure of so much privacy to untutored hands seems irresponsible and misguided.

The touching relics of the passage of a poet or novelist on this earth can never, I suppose, be numerous enough. The biographer can only be grateful for the enterprise and energy of gifted administrators and collectors and vigilant librarians. The riches are there; the embarrassment of riches is acute. Nevertheless a new dimension, and a terrible one, has been added to the writing of lives. How is the biographer to face such weight and mass and density? How is he to encompass such immense stockpiles?

III

This is a crucial question, and scholarship, I would venture to say, has not properly addressed itself to it. Man is a creature of habit; and scholars, perhaps because they are disciplined, possess deeply ingrained habits. Unlike poets and novelists, who remake their worlds daily, some scholars tend to work in a fixed world until they come to prefer it to the ceaseless inventiveness of our times. They tend often to confront the new with the tools of the old. It takes time to fashion new tools, especially those of the mind; it takes time to rethink old ways of doing things. I remember how in 1939, during the first days of the second war, everyone spoke in terms of the war of position of 1914–1918, whereas the war became above all a war of movement. So scholars facing new archives often assume that old methods are still viable. And they work out of ancient rigidities. Among such rigidities I would list the following:

1. A tendency to bog down in trivia. No distinction is made between what is primary and what is secondary (and what may even be found ultimately to be irrelevant); a tendency to treat *all* documents as if they were sacrosanct—on the ground that one never knows which may be important. Documents are indeed precious, but we must be prepared to judge, evaluate and discard.

2. A tendency to adhere rigidly to chronology instead of shuttling back and forth within the materials whenever warranted. The researcher must not be afraid to range freely in the archive.

3. A tendency to treat material in an antiquarian sense,

as if it were a series of possessions, rather than so much raw material to be ultimately refined into a narrative. This also represents failure to differentiate between the important and the trivial.

These may seem like technical matters, but they are significant symptoms of a lack of method, a lack of theory. They betray a failure to adopt a critical attitude toward an archive and a failure also to treat it as something requiring a conscious strategy on the biographer's part. How many biographers tell us in their prefaces that they are going to let their subject "speak for himself"? One knows at once what they have done. They have strung together a series of excerpts from documents and contributed no treatment or interpretation, often not even a proper connecting narrative. And then we have the other biographer, the democrat of the archive, who decides to let the reader do the biography. He usually explains in his preface that he had not presumed to interpret his materials; he has merely arranged them so the reader can form his own opinion. Most readers, we know, experience no desire to do so; they expect the biographer to do it for them. This is after all the biographer's job of work. He has seen everything there is to see; *he* should have the answers. The reader only knows as much as has been arranged for him to know. These biographical "dodges" are disingenuous. The books announce themselves as mere compilations in their opening sentence. Indeed, if a biographer feels strongly that he should let his subject speak for himself, he should refrain from writing a biography and edit his letters and papers instead.

In his history of biography Richard Altick has quoted a useful example of indiscriminate cramming of detail. It is from a chronicle of Amy Lowell's life, compiled by S. Foster Damon out of eight packing cases stuffed with correspondence and indexed scrapbooks. The humor I believe was unintended.

> The summer in Dublin [New Hampshire] was occupied chiefly with correcting the proofs of *Men, Women and Ghosts* and writing her lectures on the American poets. On July 22, she sent her car over to the MacDowell Colony to fetch the young composer and conductor, Chalmers Clifton, and a poet friend, to dinner. James Whitcomb Riley had just died; when a reporter telephoned her the news and asked for a comment, she said she was very sorry. On July 29, Carl Engel was married; she went down to Brookline for the wedding. He was another of her young men to get married (Fletcher had taken the same step not two months before); it meant the end of those informal long talks that filled evenings absolutely without regard for time. She never was wholly reconciled to the fact. In early August, she had Robinson over from the Colony, to discuss her forthcoming lecture on him. On the nineteenth she read from her poems at the Dublin Lake Club, and though depressed by their reception, was cheered by having Dorothy Foster Gilman, a new admirer, to dinner on the twentieth. On the twenty-sixth she addressed "The Out-Door Players" (Marie Ware Laughton's pupils) at Peterborough on "Poetry as a Spoken Art." Braithwaite, who came up to hear it, reported it in the *Transcript* (September 2, 1916); and Martyn Johnson, who had just bought the *Dial,* and had come to Dublin to talk things over, asked her to boil the speech down for his paper. On Labor Day her house was full in consequence of a Bazaar for the Allies.

A biography is not an engagement book. It imitates life in the way of the novelist; neither the work of fact nor the work of fiction can afford to present the reader with chaos and clutter. In the quest for a continuous and flowing story, the anarchy of the archive needs to be thoroughly and completely mastered.

IV

How are we to escape the surfeit of packing cases and scrapbooks, no matter how carefully indexed? Lytton Strachey's advice is useful: he wrote that the materials for the Victorian era are so overwhelming that the biographer and historian can only row out over the great archival lake and lower a little bucket, bring up some characteristic specimens and examine them with cautious and refined curiosity. To the plodding hoarder and clutter-biographer this may seem like an impatience with facts and dates. It is the reverse. A biographer aware of facts and dates does not seed his pages with them. A life is not a calendar although it is lived in our modern world in calendar time. He will know how to deal with the contents of the inquisitive little bucket. If he doesn't learn, he is quite likely to undergo the indignity of drowning in the dark residues of the past.

When a biographer is faced with materials which would take a lifetime to read, he needs a method and a theory of research. Our starting point might be to recognize that we must have a certain amount of knowledge before we can begin to look for the characteristic and the usable. I would submit that a biographer today has to learn a great deal about his subject before he begins reading in an archive. This is hardly necessary in older times, where one is constantly involved with fragments of knowledge. But with more recent history, that of our own time, there are distinct avenues of approach. In literary biography the material which must guide us is the writer's own work, even as we approach a statesman

through his public actions and a general through his bat-
tles. We start, in other words, with the achievement.
The works are known and often readily available. They
are the reason for the writing of a literary biography.
From them we obtain much significant and intimate
knowledge. A biographer preparing for a task begins
thus by looking at the obvious and by grasping in a broad
and open-minded way what manner of man or woman
he has encountered; and he should question also from
the first what has attracted him to this man or woman,
even as he will, as he proceeds, have to see what elements his subject possessed that were unattractive. In
this preliminary process, not only will the modern biographer form a mental image of how his subject walked
and talked and comported himself among his fellows,
but he will begin to glimpse other traits, hidden motives,
the rationalizations and the concealments of the personality.

In dealing with writers, we discover quickly enough
how their inner modes of thought were projected into
their art. One example will suffice. There has been considerable argument among American scholars as to
whether Hawthorne's solitary recluse years in Salem were
really as solitary as he makes them seem. Biographers
have sought to show him moving among men and have
even invented a highly active role for him, a secret life.
The truest answer is to be found in Hawthorne's novels,
and they should be the guide to all the Hawthorne documents. His novels deal with men and women who find
themselves outside their society and yet want to be a part
of it. I would venture to say that no matter how much
evidence might be adduced tomorrow to turn Hawthorne into a highly active man of affairs, we would still
know that he felt isolated and alone. As we read on, we

find corroboration in his notebooks, phrases in his letters, fancies in his tales which reveal a strange spiritual solitude. The theme of guilt is ever present; and while the biographer may never fathom the full meaning of this obsession, he must confront and pay close attention to Hawthorne's brooding on the misdeeds of his ancestors, for which he invited personal blame. My point is that we are forced, in the end, to draw some connection between Hawthorne's documented life and the documented private states of feeling in his work. What I am suggesting, in reality, is that if the biographer reads a writer's work carefully, he is already in possession of a significant compass to that writer's archives, because he is made aware of the singular personality who is his subject. He has seen and knows the work; and he must discover the life materials out of which it came into being. Sometimes he will at first not see deeply enough. But he will have the means to enlarge his original hypotheses and will know when to correct them and, if necessary, to discard them. By this kind of continuing psychological approach, he can arrive at the heart of a life, and outwit the raw abundance of the archive—the great attic of biography. He is better prepared to grasp character and "life-style" and to dismiss the library's necessary trivia.

I have not offered a set of rules for confronting an archive. What is required is recognition that we work in a new era of history. Archives will grow more massive; we may need teams of researchers. Computers will help. Yet I would suggest that in the final task, when the materials are being melted down, there will be parts of the archive that the biographer must see with his own eyes. One can never tell when a single phrase will light up entire chapters—a less indoctrinated researcher cannot be sensitive to that phrase or realize its implications in the same way.

When a biographer has accepted the idea of personal indoctrination by which the archive may become a place of rummage or where the little bucket becomes the tool of salvage, he will find that the spurious sinks to the bottom, the irrelevant is easily tossed aside, and the clouds of witnesses may be challenged by the writer's own distillations from the dreary masses of paper. Psychology is the greatest aid of all. The biographer equipped to understand dream logic in all its distortions and perversities, man's ability to be rational and irrational at the same time, and imaginative in self-delusion, will disengage a richer life, a life possessing the ambiguities which we all possess and of which we are deeply aware. The new biography has learned what the old could never understand: that we are self-contradicting and ambivalent, that life is neither as consistent nor as intellectual as biography would have it be, and that when we come as close as possible to character and personality and to the nature of temperament and genius, we have written the kind of biography that comes closest to truth. In the struggle with intractable materials the biographer might remember how Madame Curie and her husband melted down tons and tons of pitchblende residues over a very long period in order to arrive finally at a very small quantity of radium—the equivalent of which, in the biographical process, would be the mysterious, the hidden and seldom visible human spirit, its inner myths and the inner propulsion that carries it through our daily awakening to existence.

cess we are in a battle with our own defenses and blocked memories and self-deceptions.

In their quest, biographers lead a particular, often obsessed, life which yields its own stories and adventures. Yet in the end they must write a different story: their final adventure is the construction of their mosaic, making a whole out of disparate elements, taking the reader into their confidence. If biographers are destined to be obsessed with "fact" they also need to remind themselves of what Coleridge said—"how mean a thing a mere fact is except as seen in the light of some comprehensive truth." The biographer's moral oath has been to seek out comprehensive truth; beguilement into irrelevant byways must be resisted. The Sherlock Holmes of the library and the attic is tempted to tell the story of the hunt, rather than settle down to the judicial proceedings. The quest is easier to describe than the subject of the quest. The private biographical triumphs are "the story of the story" and one wishes more biographers would make separate books of these, or write their autobiographies rather than allow them to intrude in their particular narrative of the life they have researched. I know of only one biographer who succeeded in combining his hunt with his story. A.J.A. Symons wrote *The Quest for Corvo* as an account of his search that at the same time told the life of his quarry, that of the spurious Baron Corvo—Frederick Rolfe—the homosexual who felt he had a vocation for religion and wrote out his fantasy of becoming a pope. *The Quest for Corvo* is a fascinating journey into documents and life, unfolding the information as it is brought to the surface, and leading us in the end to the final Venetian adventures of the self-sanctifying Rolfe. It has all the charm and tension of a detective story. The danger in such biographies is that of

irrelevancy. Symons avoids this pitfall but another biography of our time, that of the Gelbs, dealing with the
life of Eugene O'Neill, illustrates the dangers of turning
biography into the story of the biographer's sleuthing.
The Gelbs, husband and wife, intruded into their biography as inquiring reporters: they described themselves
going about interviewing their witnesses; they described
the witnesses. It was a little as if in a trial one began
giving the lives of witnesses primacy over their testimony. The same kind of irrelevance can be found in
archives. Norman Holmes Pearson of Yale long ago made
public a letter from the popular novelist Hervey Allen,
which showed an author's uncomfortable solicitude for
the biographer and perhaps a certain exalted notion of
his own activities:

> I am a very methodical person in regard to records and
> correspondence [the author of *Anthony Adverse* wrote to
> Professor Pearson]. Over the years there has been an unbe-
> lievable number—thousands—of letters from people all over
> the world, literary and otherwise, and these have all been
> kept in carefully annotated and organized files, together
> with the replies. Amongst these letters are quite a number
> from most of my contemporaries. In addition to that, there
> are all the manuscripts of the several books, and the com-
> plete story of their publication,—reviews, comments, and
> all that goes with it. ... I am now engaged in arranging
> for a shed in which to store this material ... and get it all
> together with the correspondence of the war years, and the
> publication of books that have taken place since. In other
> words, to get the whole mass of material together and
> properly arranged in its sequence of monthly and yearly
> files. ... Part of this is forced upon me because I must
> have, easily available and on hand, the records of the past

years, in order to satisfy the Internal Revenue Department, which is forever pestering me with questions that must be completely and intimately answered as to why I did certain things in the past. As at the present time I am paying income taxes and agents' fees etc. etc. in some twenty-one countries, you can see how complex it is, and yet how necessary.

Posterity may not be altogether as happy as the Internal Revenue for such deference; yet what biographer or historian would want to apply the match of kindness to this shedful of papers? Boswell boasted in the opening pages of his life of Johnson that he had not melted down his materials, but had allowed his subject to speak wherever possible in his own voice. Imagine the twentieth-century biographer, groaning under his burden, making such a boast! If he followed Boswell's prescription he would have to write a massive life and what publisher—what reader, indeed—would want it? Rare are the lives in the history of the world that require such amplitude. Even Masson's *Milton* crowds the shelf as a history of Milton's time as well as of his life; and the Monypenny and Buckle *Disraeli* or the Nicolay and Hay life of Lincoln, splendid in their many-volumed detail, are in reality source books, from which other biographers write readable single-volumed lives.

We have a striking paradox when we contemplate the biographer rich in material of his subject and his starved brother handling material of the prebiographical era. The latter would give much for a few shreds of documents on the life of Shakespeare or of Marlowe. The modern writer of lives, an unwilling glutton, busy shoveling tons of paper, at moments longs for a leaner diet. Who is to say, however, which has the harder task: the biographer starved of detail who must grub for facts in the entire background of an era, or the one for whom the background is not even visible because detail clogs the foreground? There seems to be small choice; either way the past looms as a rough mountain, difficult to climb. I suspect that if one were to measure the hours of work and the reward, it would be discovered that biography is the costliest of all literary labors.

II

There is still another kind of subject for the hardworking biographer, the exact opposite of the hoarding, accumulating type who can't throw papers away. The opposite kind would seem to have had a fireplace in every room of his house, the more quickly to get rid of papers, I have an example ready at hand. I think I can describe the quest for the materials of Henry James's life with an intimacy no one can duplicate; and I suspect that this intimacy is preferable to my drawing upon examples at second hand from other biographers. I shall risk the charge of being frivolous and autobiographical in the interest of the generalizations I wish to draw. I would particularly justify my choice of Henry James on the ground that he offers us the unique picture of a novelist who, in the most premeditated fashion in the world, arranged a tug of war between himself and his future biographer.

Let us look first at the problem of James's letters.

The novelist wrote for fifty years. Few days passed without the regular stint at his desk; even when he traveled, his pen set down its record in journals, travel articles, tales, novels. At the end of his day's writing there was the dinner, the social evening, the theater, and then a late return and letters—it might be ten or fifteen in an evening—to friends, relations, acquaintances. Sometimes he wrote full, warm letters largely about his art. He wrote gossipy letters as well, but he seldom talked about himself. He could be very precise and matter-of-fact in writing to editors, publishers or literary agents. He was equally precise and acutely critical and honest if literary matters were being discussed. Concerning himself, however, the details are always general and often trivial: the intimate glimpses are few and rather guarded. His letters are remarkable for their fluency, their cordiality, their vitality and, and their "distance"; they are the overflow of a man's creativity, the surplus of his genius. They are often highly descriptive and they are nearly always filled with fine, free phrases thrown off with great liberality. He accepts an invitation: "Dearest Clare, You should have heard the peal of strident laughter with which I greeted—and treated—your question of whether I shall really turn up on Friday next; a question so solemnly and so sacredly settled in the affirmative, an intention so ardently cherished, a prospect so fondly caressed. ..." He issues an invitation: "Dearest Jocelyn, If you are miraculously able to come—on the 7th and sit through my twaddle, to feel you beautifully there will give all the pleasure in life and be an immense support, to your all-affectionate old Henry James." He describes a voyage: "I was lifted over the wide sea in the great smooth huge kind Mauretania as if I had been carried in a gigantic grandmother's bosom and the gentle giantess had made but one mighty stride of it from land to land"; or a wedding, in "a very cold church, to see my friend Mrs. Carter, married: a rather dreary occasion, with a weeping bride, a sepulchral clergyman who buried rather than married her, and a total destitution of relatives or accomplices of her own, so that she had to be given away by her late husband's brother." Or he finds the elegiac words with which to mourn his old friend, Fanny Kemble: "I am conscious of a strange bareness and a kind of evening chill as it were in the air, as if some great object that had filled it for long had left an emptiness—from displacement—to all the senses." He thanks a distinguished authoress (Sara Orne Jewett) for sending him her book: "It would take me some time to disembroil the tangle of saying to you at once how I appreciated the charming touch, tact and taste of this ingenious exercise, and how little I am in sympathy with experiments of its general (to my sense) misguided stamp. . . . There I am— yet I won't do you the outrage as a fellow craftsman and a woman of genius and courage, to suppose you not as conscious as I am myself of all that, in these questions of art and truth and sincerity, is beyond the mere twaddle of graciousness."

The mere twaddle of graciousness. So many of Henry James's letters were that, a distribution of accolades and muted strictures, a wrapping of sharp criticism in the soft cushions of kindness. James's letters can be very misleading. Their extravagant affection sometimes suggests closer friendship than actually existed; their elaborate, friendly irony masks deeper feelings, an intention to express the truth at all costs and yet to pad it out with gentle words. Read in isolation or out of context, these letters are sown with pitfalls. Elaborate praise in one sentence is often offered as prelude for sharp criticisms, a verbal pat on the back sometimes becomes a subterfuge for a sound boxing of artistic ears. It is only by a long and careful process of study of the different qualities of friendship expressed in hundreds of James's letters—I should say thousands—that I have found it possible to sort out the meaning of his relationships with his correspondents and to isolate from the "mere twaddle of graciousness" those communications which speak for the more intimate Henry James. He was conscious early of the claims of posterity. He often enjoined his correspondents to "burn this, please, burn, burn." I find these particular words in a letter to his sister Alice. The fact that I am able to quote them indicates what happened. Few lit the destructive match. Nearly everyone preserved Henry James's letters.

I find them on all sides: one turned up in Honolulu recently, another in Finland. And each owner, even now, although removed from the recipients, seems to discern in them particular qualities, confidential and intimate. Yet how deceptive this can be! For in this biographical abundance much more is concealed than revealed. The letters are a part of the novelist's work, of his literary self, a part of his capacity for playing out personal relations as a great game of life ... but we find indeed that only a part of James's life is in them, especially when we compare them with the letters of the romantic poets, those who tore their passions to tatters, in particular on the Gallic side of the Channel. Not so in the letters of the American novelist: we seem indeed to watch him as he watches himself in a mirror.

A man so cautious left no love letters: at least so far none have been found; indeed, a man so cautious apparently did not allow himself to be in love. And when a man is as self-concealing as this, where is the writer of his life to find him? The biographer is confronted with an elaborate, organized game of hide-and-seek or hunt-the-author. James's deliberate effort to thwart his future biographer can be discovered on every side. "Artists," he wrote when he was twenty-nine, "as time goes on will be likely to take the alarm, empty their table drawers and level the approaches to their privacy. The critics, psychologists and gossip-mongers may then glean amid the stubble." Three years later, when his first novel is being serialized in the *Atlantic Monthly,* he returns to the same theme: "A man has certainly a right to determine what the world shall know of him and what it shall not; the world's natural curiosity to the contrary notwithstanding," and he adds that there should be a "certain sanctity in all appeals to the generosity and forbearance of posterity, and that a man's table drawers and pockets should not be turned inside out."

What steps did Henry James take to keep his table drawers and pockets from prying biographical hands? For one thing, he had a secret drawer in one of his seven desks; but when it was discovered after his death it yielded a gout remedy and a prescription for eyeglasses! Wherever he turns, the biographer stumbles upon an ironic mockery, a kind of subterranean laughter—at the biographer! Henry James is coy in his prefaces about the magazines in which his work first appeared. He revises his early writings and alters the first person "I" to the more general "one." He hedges certain passages of his autobiographies with qualifications. The euphemism becomes a constant instrument of expression. And then there is the direct attack upon the past.

Early in the new century James's health gave him some concern. One day he heaped his correspondence of forty years upon a great roaring fire in his garden at Lamb House, in Sussex, and watched its progress from paper to ash, obeying "the law that I have made tolerably absolute these last years as I myself grow older and think more of my latter end: the law of not leaving personal and private documents at the mercy of any accidents, or even of my executors! I kept almost all letters for years—till my receptacles could no longer hold them;

then I made a gigantic bonfire and have been easier in mind since." Like his own character in "The Aspern Papers," he could have boasted, "I have done the great thing." The "great thing" was the burning of the Aspern papers, the love letters of the famous poet, one by one, in the kitchen stove. It is quite clear that Henry James, warming his hands by the fire at Lamb House, would have exclaimed with Dickens who lit a similar blaze at Gad's Hill: "Would to God every letter I have ever written were on that pile." But here resides a great irony. While Dickens and James, both prolific letter writers, burned letters that would have illuminated many other lives and done service in other biographies, they could do little about those letters which illuminate their own and which turn up even now in such numbers.

Henry James was acutely conscious of having lived into the new age of journalism and its excessive curiosity about the living great. His private life was private indeed. He could push secrecy to a fine art. He confided in no one. His open, ritualistic life was a mask, and in a late essay on George Sand he repeated in more elaborate form what he had said as a young man and also embodied in one of his late ghostly tales, "The Real Right Thing." This tale has a biographer-hero who in the end finds the ghost of his subject planted in the doorway of the study, warning him to abandon his project. In the essay on George Sand, James deplored—and not without some relish—the manner in which the prolific lady's love affairs were unscrambled in public and the way in which her letters of passion, and those of Chopin and Musset, were given to the world. At the same time a mischievous and slightly boastful note creeps in. He would be careful not to reveal himself. No one would turn *his* pockets inside out.

He begins the essay by observing that to leave every-thing to the biographer, to make his task easy, is so to speak, to remove one's clothes to the public gaze, and when one has laid bare one's life, as George Sand and her biographer did, what was there left to know? "When we meet on the broad highway the rueful denuded fig-ure we need some presence of mind to decide whether to cut it dead or to lead it gently home, and meanwhile the fatal complication occurs. We have *seen,* in a flash of our own wit, and mystery has fled with a shriek." He goes on to say that the writer does suffer accidents; he can't hide all his secrets; and there are many kinds of encounters on the broad highways of literature and life. What is to be done? With that need for putting every-thing in order—the house of fiction as the house of life—Henry James suggests that the biographic quest be orga-nized. "The general guarantee in a noisy world," he says, "lies, I judge, not so much in any hope of really averting them [the encounters] as in a regular organisation of the struggle." The subject of a biography has in the past left things too much to luck. It is up to him to create the ground for a more equal conflict. And he continues:

The reporter and the reported have duly and equally to understand that they carry their life in their hands. There are secrets for privacy and silence; let them only be culti-vated on the part of the hunted creature with even half the method with which the love of sport—or call it the historic sense—is cultivated on the part of the investigator. They have been left too much to the natural, the instinctive man; but they will be twice as effective after it begins to be observed that they may take their place among the triumphs of civilisation. Then at last the game will be fair and the two forces face to face; it will be "pull devil, pull tailor," and the hardest pull will doubtless provide the happiest result. Then the cunning of the inquirer, envenomed with resistance, will exceed in subtlety and ferocity anything we today conceive, and the pale forewarned victim, with every track covered, every paper burnt and every letter unanswered, will, in the tower of art, the invulnerable granite, stand, without a sally, the siege of all the years.

The tower of art, the invulnerable granite, the siege of the years: this is Henry James's challenge to posterity—and to his biographer!

III

Every track covered, every paper burnt and—subtlest twist of all—every letter unanswered! We are offered by such a stroke the silence of the tomb. One can attempt to match wits with covered tracks and burnt papers; but out of silence there can come only silence. And yet not all papers do get burned; not every track can remain covered; not every letter can remain unanswered. The subject of a biography may throw up roadblocks, but can he ever completely stop the traffic?

There exists, for instance, a monograph on angina pectoris by the late Sir James Mackenzie, who was not only a great cardiac authority, but a wise and gifted healer. His little book, written for the members of his profession, is the last place in the world that we would look for biographical material concerning an American novelist. Yet in this medical volume, never intended for literary biographers, I one day found the following passage to which I was led by a clue that had quite fortuitously come to me. The passage is worth quoting from beginning to end:

I was once consulted by a distinguished novelist. Just before he came to see me I had read one of his short stories, in which an account was given of an extraordinary occurrence that happened to two children. Several scenes were recounted in which these children seemed to hold converse with invisible people, after which they were greatly upset. After one occasion one of them turned and fled, screaming with terror, and died in the arms of the narrator of the story. After my examination of the novelist I referred to this story and said to him "You did not explain the nature of the mysterious interviews." He at once expounded to me the principles on which to create a mystery. So long as the events are veiled the imagination will run riot and depict all sorts of horrors, but as soon as the veil is lifted, all mystery disappears and with it the sense of terror.

I tapped him on the chest and said "It is the same with you, it is the mystery that is making you ill. You think that you have angina pectoris, and you are frightened lest you should die suddenly. Now, let me explain to you the real matters. You are sixty-six years of age. You have the changes in your body which are coincident with your time of life. It happens that the changes in the arteries of your heart are a little more advanced than those of your brain, or in your legs. It simply follows that if you be more judicious in your living, and give your heart less work to do, there is no reason why you should not reach the ordinary span of human life." He was greatly cheered by this way of putting the matter and remained in good health, except that his powers of locomotion became more restricted and he died at the age of seventy-two from cerebral embolism.

The description of the story sounds very much like "The Turn of the Screw" and the explanation of how to keep events veiled and allow the reader's imagination to "run riot" corresponds to Henry James's description of his formula for "horror" and evil in his preface to that ghostly tale. Moreover, James's correspondence shows that in 1909 he was worried about his health and consulted physicians. This year fits the doctor's description of his novelist patient's age, sixty-six. Also we know that Henry James died at seventy-two of cerebral embolism. But the novelist might reply to us: "You have no *absolute* proof!"—and he might say other rather forceful things as well about the biographical invasion of consulting room privacy. "You have no absolute proof," he might say, "for I am not mentioned by name." Well, it so happens that there is proof which comes as close to being absolute as any proof can. Discreet as Sir James Mackenzie was, his case history (Case 97), buried in this volume among many other such histories, did not escape the eye of Dr. Harold L. Rypins, a professor of medicine in Albany Medical School, with a penchant for literary study. Dr. Rypins wrote a letter to Sir James, pointing out that the novelist had been dead for several years, and inquired whether the secrets of the consulting room, already partly divulged, might not be further unveiled. "You are quite right," replied Sir James in a letter which I have seen, "and it was "The Turn of the Screw" to which I referred. After our first interview we became very friendly and he frequently visited me, particularly when depressed."

Every track covered?

In his memoirs Henry James describes how he moved into a little room near Harvard in 1862 when he was nineteen and began to write short stories. Then, with his characteristic coyness in such matters, he throws these words at his biographer: "Nothing would induce me to name the periodical on whose protracted silence I had . . . begun to hang with my own treasures of reserve to match it." James seemed to believe that his early writings were beyond recovery. Did not anonymity provide a sheltering cloak? Would it not cast a perpetual doubt for any future wielders of the bibliographical pickax and spade? He little dreamed that nearly all his anonymous contributions to the *Nation*—book reviews, travel articles and literary notes—would some day be known because an account book, listing payments for articles, would be preserved by one of the *Nation's* editors. But exasperating evidence began to appear in recent years that buried prose existed, written before those articles were discovered in 1907 by Le Roy Phillips in his *Nation* researches. Among the papers relating to Henry James's brothers I found a letter from Garth Wilkinson James of December 1864 written from the Civil War front to the elder Henry James saying: "Tell Harry that I am waiting anxiously for his 'next.' I can find a large sale for any blood and thunder tale among the darks." And long ago T. S. Perry, the friend of James's adolescent years, testified that the would-be novelist wrote early tales in Newport in which the heroes were villains and the heroines were positively dripping lurid crimes and seemed to have read Balzac in their cradles.

Publication in 1950 of James's letters to Perry offered further evidence. In March of 1864, a year before the appearance of James's first signed story in the *Atlantic Monthly,* the novice in letters was writing to Perry that the printer's devil had been knocking at his door. "You know a literary man can't call his time his own." The literary man added that he was sending a story to the *Atlantic* and giving Perry's address as the place to which the acceptance or rejection would be sent. "I cannot again stand the pressure of avowed authorship (for the present) and their answer could not come here unobserved.

Do not speak to Willie of this." If Henry James's sensitivity to fraternal teasing is here revealed—"Willie" being his elder brother, William James, who was to become the eminent psychologist and philosopher—there is also revealed an important fact: avowed authorship—"again."

But where, in what strange waters, is the biographer to fish for this avowed author? "Nothing would induce me to name the periodical," Henry wrote half a century later. The investigative biographer or bibliographer can only set such things aside and hope for some happy accident. Meanwhile there are always other problems. One was to obtain certain letters I had long wanted, written to a Venetian hostess, an American lady, who was for many years a friend of Henry James's and of Robert Browning's. I had learned that they were in possession of that lady's daughter, aged ninety-two, who lived in a Renaissance palace in Florence. These elements sound rather like Henry James's own tale of "The Aspern Papers." But unlike the "publishing scoundrel" of that story, I was unable to journey to Florence and sit on the doorstep of the modern Juliana in the hope of obtaining a glimpse of the letters. Instead I invoked the good offices of a relative of the Florentine lady who lived in New York and who was on her way to Italy.

Weeks elapsed. I completed the manuscript of my biography of Henry James's early years and cleared my cluttered table preparatory to cluttering it again with the materials for the second volume—but with an acute sense that there were certain loose ends perhaps never to be properly tied together. One day I received a telephone call. My ambassadress had returned. She had copied certain letters for me. I saw, on reading them, that they would serve my later needs. But during my talk with her she quite casually mentioned that her grandmother had lived in Newport and had been a neighbor of the Jameses. She had found her grandmother's letters to her father. Did I think there might be material for me in this correspondence? She would look through the accumulation, one never could tell what an old bundle of letters might reveal. And so it was that early one November morning, when my manuscript had already been dispatched to my publisher, I received another telephone call from this amiable and helpful lady. She had found a solitary reference to young Harry James in her grandmother's letters and she read from a letter dated 29 February 1864: "Henry James has published a story in the February Continental called a Tragedy of Errors. Read it." Thus an old letter, written by an unobtrusive bystander, a Newport neighbor, to her son, divulged what nothing would have induced the novelist to divulge. The *Continental Monthly,* in its bound volume at the New York Public Library, was as crisp and new as if published yesterday. Sure enough, a story called "A Tragedy of Error," unsigned, appeared in the February 1864 issue, a month before James spoke of his "avowed authorship." It fitted Perry's description and Wilky James's; it was lurid blood-and-thunder stuff; it was seasoned with those French phrases Henry delighted in using during his formative years; it was set in France; the heroine was sufficiently Balzacian—or perhaps had a George Sand touch about her: in theme, style, substance, it is a primitive Henry James story.

Every track covered?

By what circuitous routes we travel in the biographical maze! A chance encounter in a drawing room with the widow of the Albany doctor led me to the letter from Sir James Mackenzie; an appeal for certain Venetian letters brought me a much more valuable Newport letter. Such are the happy accidents of the quest, and if there are unwritten letters—or unanswered letters—there appear to be letter-writing neighbors. Perhaps the cunning of the inquirer is ferocious, as Henry James said; but let us remember that the art of the biographer does not lie wholly in the uncovering of tracks. The particular skill of Sherlock Holmes, in the days before fictional detectives became sadists and resorted to violence and blackmail to solve crimes, lay not so much in observing the bits of mud on the boots of the visitor, or evaluating an interlocutor from his habits of dress, or reading between the lines of what he was saying. It lay in his power of induction, his imaginative grasp of his materials, his ability to deduce the unknown from the known. So the biographer must not be content to be merely Sherlock Holmes, the sleuth. He must possess Holmes's capacity for synthesis and ratiocination. To stumble upon James's visit to the consulting room of Sir James Mackenzie was a rare bit of luck; but it is what transpired between James and Mackenzie, and how it relates to James's work, that is important, and unless the necessary connections are made, all that we have is a rather charming anecdote. To have stumbled on the anonymous story is but a lucky accident, due to chance as much as to persistence. The meaning of that story, its value to us as part of James's late adolescence, or as art, partake of the essential task of the biographer. The mass of documents on the worktable remains a mass, inert, paper and words, to which we have added but one more document by uncovering this particular track. It is the arrangement of these documents and their distillation into a homogeneous, synthetic whole that provide the real test of modern literary biography in the sense in which I think it should be written.

Did the discovery of this early story make necessary any change in my book, since I had already completed it when the happy accident of its finding occurred? The question should be answered. "A Tragedy of Error" is about a strong, determined Frenchwoman who takes a lover during her husband's absence in America and who, on learning of his impending return, plots with a fisherman to have him drowned.

> "You want me to finish him in the boat?"
> No answer.
> "Is he an old man?"
> Hortense shook her head faintly.
> "My age?"
> She nodded.
> *"Sapristi!* it isn't so easy."
> "He can't swim," said Hortense, without looking up, ·
> "he—is lame."
> *"Nom de dieu."* The boatman dropped his hands.

A writer's first story is often more transparently autobiographical than his later work. In this case I had only to insert a brief analysis of the tale at the proper chronological moment. It confirmed my original decision to devote the early pages of the book to a more detailed account of the elder Henry James's lameness than had hitherto been given—he lost a leg when he was thirteen—and to show how deep an impression the father's accident had made on his son; and also how the son's vision from childhood had been of a father who, for all his vividness and charm, was a vacillating individual while his wife gave an impression to her children of a strength and determination almost masculine. That understanding had been arrived at earlier from a reading of James's work. The citadel of granite yielded these observations. The

[127

new track uncovered confirmed, for an earlier stage, what is quite apparent in later evidence. The pattern of the work had yielded a pattern of the life.

And this brings me to the next problem in our inquiry into the nature of literary biography. The pile of documents has now been assembled. Great quantities of paper have been set aside as of little use. The essential diaries and writings, the important letters and notebooks, everything that throws light upon the character and the personality and the artistic imagination, is there for us to use. The writer's works have been closely read and reread—the biographer is always reading them, he can never have enough of them. Now, in particular, the biographer's critical faculties come into play. They have been operative all the time, inevitably, as he has gone through his materials. But in the process of sorting, arranging, preparing to write, he must be ready to function as a critic of literature as well as a literary historian. He is called upon for an awareness of certain standards, a feeling for form, and an understanding of the nature of the work itself. He must also have a profound understanding of what constitutes testimony, what may be held to be valid and invalid. He has been interrogating clouds of witnesses almost as if he were a studious lawyer bent not upon prosecuting anyone, but arriving at the truth. The question of the biographer's relation to "criticism" is an integral part of any literary life.

Criticism

THE MATERIAL is gathered. The great table, piled high with documents, confronts the biographer. On his shelves he has assembled, row upon row, the works of the writer whose life he wishes to recover and to place within a book. Sometimes there are only a few works, as with James Joyce, and sometimes, as with poets, there is only the single volume of verses. Strange thought in such instances: that there should be such a weight of paper to surround one book—one thinks of John Keats—so much material to set beside the words in which the poet crystallized experience.

How different is the critic's task! His table, in contrast to the biographer's, is uncluttered. No birth certificates, no deeds, no letters, no diaries, no excess literary baggage: only the works, the poems or the novels or the plays, to be read and reread, pondered and analyzed, in a clear literary light, a communion between words and print and a critical intelligence, greater or less, as intelligences go. The critic, when he is performing an exclusive function of appraisal, need not be a biographer, although there are few critics who do not cast at least a sidelong glance at a literary life. The literary biographer, however, must at every moment of his task be a critic. His is an act of continual and unceasing criticism.

[129

The task begins with the reading and evaluation of the subject's work; it extends to that other form of criticism, the weighing and evaluation of evidence, a function legalistic or juridical, requiring hardheaded logic, a good sense of reality, and an imagination perhaps akin to the poet's, although functioning in matters at times rather prosaic. Both forms of criticism are not in reality divorced from each other: they function simultaneously and call for a constant and studious watchfulness.

I

The critical reading of the works involves for the biographer a complete knowledge of them; he must steep himself in them until he can offer an explication of every text; he must be aware of the way the author uses the materials of his craft and appreciate formal structure and the relation of work to work; he must possess and cultivate all the sensitivities of the critic and what we might call the *critical* imagination. The critic and the biographer must see the particular and the general, the story itself and the myth of which it may be a part. They gather up the images and symbols of the poet, or in fiction the design, the range, the matter, the manner, the creation of characters, their projection and their relations—gather them up to attach them to tradition and discipline and influence, and determine their essential pattern and meaning. The biographer enters into the heart of each piece of writing as if it were the only work ever written; and as he reads and studies it, he relates it to the psyche that gave it birth. He discovers recurrent images and recurrent modes of thought; patterns have a way of repeating themselves, for each writer has his own images and his own language and his own chain of fantasy; there is no writer, no matter how rich and varied his imagination, who does not possess his individual world of words and his peculiar vision of reality. One need not venture far into the earlier T. S. Eliot to discover how often dry bones and windy spaces, rats and desiccation spring from his vision into verbal structure, and how characteristically he sees streets, cities, people within them. There is no poet or prose writer who forges a style and achieves transcendent utterance without stamping his literary effigy on both sides of every coin he mints. A style, it has been said, is a writer's passport to posterity. This is another way of saying that the style is the man. The biographer can argue, with equal validity, that the man is the style. Indeed this is what he is trying to demonstrate.

In this reading of the works in a fashion as closely critical as that of any of our most addicted critics, the biographer reminds himself, in the light of the twentieth century's exploration of the psyche, that every comma, every period, every inflection, every word has been placed on the page by the living, glowing, creating being. If he reads the words of the novelist, he soon begins to see that certain types of story—regardless of the adventitious circumstances of creation—certain significant characters, certain solutions and certain ethical views—have a way of recurring, always in new and artful disguises. However much a great work is independent of its creator, and may be judged independently, invisible threads remain—many more than anyone can discover and disentangle—which bind it to the fashioning mind. There is a little story which charmingly illustrates this elementary point, so important in explaining the biographical approach to art and to life. It is that of a young woman who in the early dawn dreamt that the wrapped and silent figure of a man came to the foot of her bed and stood looking at her. Her alarm was great. As she drew the bedclothes about her with—one may well imagine—trembling hands, she fairly screamed: "Oh my goodness, what are you going to do to me?" Whereupon the figure broke his stony silence to reply, without moving: "I don't know, lady. It's *you* who are having the dream."

We dream our own dreams. No one else dreams them for us. No one puts them into our heads. Indeed everything we put into the dreams, however brilliant or absurd, pleasant or painful, is the work of our unconscious imagination. When a writer sits down to write, all his past sits behind his pen. His muscles and his nerves, and above all his emotions—and no one else's—drive the pen across the page. And this one self driving the pen is many selves, some of them very contradictory. "A biography is considered complete," observed Virginia Woolf, "if it merely accounts for six or seven selves whereas a person may well have as many thousand." Yes, but we must remember they all belong to the one person: and it is this person who is sought by the biographer.

Woolf, who wrote many wise words about the art of biography, also observed that "every secret of a writer's soul, experience of his life, every quality of his mind is written large in his works, yet we require critics to explain the one and biographers to expound the other." There is a rueful note in this coupling of critics and biographers, the note of a writer who would have the work be self-sufficient—beyond criticism, beyond biography—but who is well aware that this cannot be. Virginia Woolf was expressing a wish and compounding an irony rather than asserting the inviolability of the artist's work. It is illuminating, however, to ask ourselves, in pondering her words, why the critic and the biographer are needed, since their function is precisely to pluck out "every secret of a writer's soul" and rob the work of all its mystery. They tend to make it as plain and as clear as daylight, so that the reader may appreciate its complexity and experience it the more deeply. *Every secret of a writer's soul, every quality of his mind.* The act of imaginative writing is an act of expression and only incidentally an act of communication. The inner promptings to which a writer listens cannot remain within; they seek an issue, they must emerge; and they usually do in the form of narratives—prose, lyrical, dramatic—tissued out of past experience and formed in a literary tradition. So long as these suggest the secrets of a writer's soul and the quality of his mind, as they must, the curious reader, sharing the writer's experience, will want to learn the secret and pierce to the heart of the mystery.

"In our opinion," wrote Henry James, "the life and the works are two very different matters, and an intimate knowledge of the one is not at all necessary for the genial enjoyment of the other. A writer who gives us his works is not obliged to throw his life after them, as is very apt to be assumed by persons who fail to perceive that one of the most interesting pursuits in the world is to read between the lines of the best literature." To read between the lines of the best literature can indeed be one of the most absorbing pursuits in the world: to catch the flickering vision behind the metaphor, to touch the pulse of the hand that holds the pen—this is what the biographer attempts, although he knows that at best he will capture only certain moments, and largely echoes. The critic reads to expound and expatiate upon the words that issued from the pen: the biographer does this always to discover the particular mind and body that drove the pen in the creative act.

I knew once in Paris a very old lady who had been a minor poet among the Victorians. She used to sit at eighty near the smiling portrait of herself painted by Sargent when she was twenty and talk, in the years between the two wars, as if she had seen Browning the day before yesterday and as if Walter Pater had tipped his hat to her that very morning when she opened her shutters and saw him passing in the street. In the preface to her collected poems, A. Mary F. Robinson, whom I knew as Madame Duclaux, wrote: "My life has been an Ode, of which these pages are scattered fragments. If ever I have escaped from its tranquil sequences, it has been but for an instant and through some partial opening of the gates of Imagination, set in movement by some incident in real life, or some episode of my reading. I have never been able to write about what was not known to me and near." This is vivid testimony from a woman of sensitivity and of strong literary impulse, to the visible ties that bind a poet to his poems.

With a major poet such as William Butler Yeats, his testimony is written large in his works. Many of his poems are autobiographical: more than half a hundred, set down over as many years, are inspired by his frustrated love for Maude Gonne; and constituting a veritable gloss to the poems are his remarkable *Autobiographies,* which provide them, as Douglas Bush said, with "a heavy scaffolding of biographical information." Yeats dedicated the biographies "to those few people mainly personal friends who have read all that I have written." These words suggest that he felt the testimony of the *Autobiographies* to be no less a part of the poet than the poems themselves. This seems to me to be the burden of his *Ego Dominus Tuus:*

> The chief imagination of Christendom,
> Dante Alighieri, so utterly found himself
> That he has made that hollow face of his
> More plain to the mind's eye than any face
> But that of Christ.

"There is always a living face behind the mask," Yeats once wrote in his diary. This is another way of saying that there must always be, inevitably, a poet behind a poem.

Yeats recognized that writers must accept from posterity the writing of their lives. "We may come to think," wrote Yeats, "that nothing exists but a stream of souls, that all knowledge is biography." And he wrote:

I have no sympathy with the mid-Victorian [and we might add modern] thought to which Tennyson gave his support, that a poet's life concerns nobody but himself. A poet is by the very nature of things, a man who lives with entire sincerity, or rather, the better his poetry the more sincere his life. His life is an experiment in living and those that come after have a right to know it. Above all it is necessary that the lyric poet's life should be known, that we should understand that his poetry is no rootless flower, but the speech of a man, that it is no little thing to achieve anything in any art, to stand alone perhaps for many years, to go a path no other man has gone, to accept one's own thoughts when the thought of others has the authority of the world behind it ... to give one's life as well as one's words, which are so much nearer to one's own soul, to the criticism of the world.

II

The first type of criticism practiced by the biographer involves a full examination of the substance, the aesthetic qualities, the fiber of a work of art, in the attempt to recover the mind and the pulse-beat of its creator. Of the second type of criticism—the judicial—there is much that could be said. It is of a more technical order. The biographer is called upon to impose logic and coherence upon the heterogeneous mass of facts he has assembled, recognizing that in the life he is pursuing they seemed quite arbitrary and, on occasion, illogical. Woolf felt distinctly that biographers were inclined to be excessively compulsive. She speaks of that "riot and confusion of the passions and emotions which every good biographer detests." I think that she is mocking even more than mere biographical tidiness. She is criticizing biography for its failure to engage itself sufficiently in the emotional life of its subject; she believes that it concerns itself too much with those dry facts which we can read in condensed form in any *Who's Who* or biographical dictionary.

Biography, when it is seriously written, is never afraid of emotion or passion. The biographer is aware how elusive and transitory some passions can be: and knows equally how passions concealed among archival papers are faded sometimes beyond recognition when held up under the lamplight. Endless resource and patience is required to recover the state of the subject's feelings after these have coalesced into a poem or been transferred to a group of characters in a novel. The complete state can never be recovered; and it was on this ground that Wystan Auden decided that biography was a fruitless pursuit; and to some extent T.S. Eliot agreed. Both seemed to wish for a complete recovery of the ecstasies and pains of creation. They could perhaps still remember in some dim and precious emotion their own. Biographers recognize such limitations and know how much is irrecoverable. The need to disengage some picture, some emotion or even some stray vapor from the text is a part of their creative *élan*. If criticism can attempt this, there is no reason to deny it to biography.

"There is always a living face behind the mask." If we ponder Yeats's words and accept the biographer's claim that a poet's or novelist's life is inextricably woven into the work, it becomes difficult to take the rigid view of certain critics who demanded—especially during the time of the "New Criticism"—an absolute divorce between biography and criticism. When Samson, in Milton's soaring classical tragedy, says in anguish

O dark, dark, dark amid the blaze of noon

the words describe Milton's blindness as well as Samson's. And when Professor Douglas Bush spoke of this as "impersonal art charged with personal meaning," he expressed not only an irony but offered a critical observation infinitely richer and more truthful than that of the critics who laboriously confined themselves to the verbal felicity and rhetorical power of this line. (I am reminded at this juncture of an evening I had with I.A. Richards once when he accused me with his warm and fierce Welsh intensity of trying to read Henry James's anxieties between the lines of his ghost story "The Turn of the Screw." When I argued that the story was much more than an artifact, that it expressed authorial nightmare, Richards exploded with "No biography! No biography! Stick to the text." And a few minutes later he started explaining that A.C. Benson had told him how sensitive Henry James was to various readings of his ghostly tale and that this explained all the euphemisms he used when asked about it. No biography indeed!)

T. S. Eliot, in his admirably leisurely prose, remarks that

Comparison and analysis needs only the cadavers on the table; but interpretation is always producing parts of the body from its pockets, and fixing them in place. And any book, any essay, any notes in *Notes and Queries,* which produces a fact even of the lowest order about a work of art is a better piece of work than nine-tenths of the most pretentious critical journalism in journals or in books. We assume, of course, that we are masters and not servants of facts, and that we know that the discovery of Shakespeare's laundry bills would not be of much use to us; but we must always reserve final judgment as to the futility of the research which has discovered them, in the possibility that some geinus will appear who will know of a use to which to put them.

Eliot goes on to say that fact cannot corrupt taste and that the real corrupters are those who supply opinion or fancy. The votaries of opinion and fancy would do well to hearken to the biographer who can materially assist them. Faced with modern art—the surrealist poem, the abstract painting, the intricate composite mythology of works such as *Finnegans Wake*—criticism finds itself admittedly forced, sometimes in a rage of bafflement, into speculation or inarticulateness. When art becomes abstract to this degree, the artist is speaking wholly from his private world and in his particular language; and any critic who tries to read his meaning by any other process than the biographical indulges in guesswork and heaps his own work of art upon the edifice of the other: projects his own feelings and discusses only his relationship to the work. Where abundant material is available, the biographer can offer a reasonably clear understanding of the creator, and our understanding of that personage should make his work more intelligible. Only by ascertaining what the symbols and myths meant to the artist in such instances can we hope to arrive at an accurate deciphering of the symbolic code, the intricate messages of imagery, metaphor, the constant analogies of the imagination.

III

I have always felt that one of the most valuable statements in behalf of the uses of biography in criticism was made by Sainte-Beuve who, by some of the present-day definitions, would be considered no critic at all, for he relied so much upon the tone and "flavor" of the poet in his poetry, or the personality expressed in a novel. He set down, a long time ago, certain words which sum up what I have been attempting to say. They may be found in the second of his *Causeries* on Chateaubriand in the third volume of his *Nouveaux Lundis*. He wrote:

> Literature, literary creation, is not distinct or separable, for me, from the rest of the man [or woman]. . . . I may taste a work, but it is difficult for me to judge it independently of my knowledge of the man himself; and I will say willingly, *tel arbre tel fruit*. Literary study leads me thus quite naturally to the study of the mind.

All of modern psychology confirms this view. More and more biographers are learning to read the inner message of an artist's words and to see that emotions translated

[139

into images and symbols are in reality biographical statements. Yeats's powerful anger at his aging is expressed in a series of poems—indeed his finest work. This was the best and most sincere way in which he could give voice to his terrible rage. Every novel Dickens or Henry James wrote reflects the particular life they were leading during the writing of their fictions. The silliest kind of biography is that which tries to discover a one-for-one likeness between streets and buildings, incidents and friendships, and certain events in a writer's life. Some of these may figure in the fiction or poem as in *Ulysses* where Joyce was putting the actual Dublin into his mock-epic. But when criticism turns to the relation of the *Odyssey* to the novel Joyce wrote, it is writing biography quite as much as criticism. And when a poet sets down a certain melancholy in his poem we know that this melancholy is rarely factitious. When Browning or Eliot give a voice to a dramatic personage, they may be constructing "impersonal" characters, but the emotions they breathe into these characters are a distillation of their own, transformations into poetic stance of their sensibilities. The very characters they choose are the children of their creative minds. Henry James explained this in a single sentence I have often quoted: "The artist is present in every page of every book from which he sought so assiduously to eliminate himself." This is the presence that becomes the subject of a literary biography. And to discover this presence the biographer doubles as a critic. What I say applies equally to the actions and doings of soldiers and statesmen whose texts, however, are perhaps easier to fathom since they are most often written in expository prose.

At the risk of seeming to turn the tables, I am inclined to say that criticism is most often one of the most interesting forms of biography. The attempt to characterize a work ends by characterizing its author. When we explore a text we explore a mind and its passions and beliefs. There is no structure of words that is not filled with emotion (or triggered by an emotion or an attempt to suppress or rationalize an emotion), and whoever creates the structure of words is writing a covert confession. Writing can rarely occur without feeling. Even hacks deal in emotional stuff; and nothing is more emotional than a president delivering a speech to a nation. Literary biography is criticism of the most valuable kind. It relates a text to the human sources from which it sprang. The quest for the "impersonal" in art is a delusion created by artists who, quite naturally, prefer the disguises bestowed on them constantly by their imagination.

Psychoanalysis

A BIOGRAPHY, said Sigmund Freud, is justified under two conditions: "first, if the subject has had a share in important generally interesting events; second, as a psychological study." Biography has reluctantly accepted the second condition. It has tended to write about individual achievements rather than explore their genesis; it has taken for granted the existence of genius but has not tried to understand the nature of genius. Freud himself admitted that psychology could not yield us all the roots and core of the human imagination, but he believed that certain psychoanalytical concepts were applicable to life-writing about creative beings, that it is possible to recognize some of the motivating forces in the artist, the soldier or the statesman and explore their behavior. Above all he provided us, in his studies of the psychopathology of everyday life, with insights into the unconscious promptings which exist within human conduct and energy. His readings of the role of the "unconscious," projected through dream and fantasy, provided an entire new province for biographical research and a quest for the psychological evidence residing within much other evidence confronting biographers. Biography to this day has been fearful and often disrespectful of psychology;

its resistance is a part of the universal resistance Freud encountered.

We need not go into the uneasy history of the relation between biography and psychology. Freud and his successors opened up biography to new modes of perception, known long ago to men of the highest literary imagination even though they did not formulate a discipline. Coleridge understood the nature of man's dream work: and it was he who first used the word *psychoanalytic* and also *psychosomatic*. He was not describing therapies—nonexistent then—but the glimpses he had into his own unconscious. Dickens saw in our dream life "the origin of all fable and allegory," and Dostoevsky understood that dreams were in reality emotions woven into symbolic story. Hypnosis long before Freud's studies with Charcot revealed the existence of a hidden level of being unknown to conscious being. William and Henry James clearly understood concealed motivations—the ways in which exuberance could be a cover-up for depression, or benign gestures could conceal aggression. Henry James spoke early in the twentieth century of "the deep well of unconscious cerebration" and after a nervous breakdown in 1910 consulted the Boston psychiatrist James J. Putnam, founder of the American Psychoanalytic Association who was familiar with Freudianism and corresponded with him. During the ensuing decade Van Wyck Brooks and Edmund Wilson, both as a consequence of exposure to therapy, used the insights afforded them in their biographical-critical writings without always being aware of the possibilities of interdisciplinary fusion. Wilson, however, in some of his biographical essays, such as those on Dickens or Lincoln, grasped the language of the unconscious. So did Lytton Strachey, who might be called the father of "psychobiography" if we want to use that cumbersome term which describes technique rather than form. Through his brother James Strachey, who had been analyzed by Freud (and later translated his works), Lytton Strachey had an indirect pipeline to Vienna. Freud wrote to Strachey to congratulate him on his *Elizabeth and Essex* and spoke of "the incompleteness of our knowledge and the clumsiness of our synthesis." He praised Strachey for his "boldness and discretion" and particularly his use of details of Elizabeth's childhood.

The general hostility to the new biographers who "psychologized" had a certain validity. A biographer learns next to nothing about psychoanalysis by getting it out of books; and the popularized ego psychology of Erik Erikson or the often ill-informed papers in the professional journals were hardly adequate sources for dealing with particular inner lives. The more successful biographies were written by those who had themselves been exposed to analysis but who often confused their therapy with the materials they were handling. Much of the confusion lay in the failure to distinguish between conscious and rationalized motivations and the promptings of the unconscious. Old school academics talked always about conscious matters; these seemed to have little to do with the devious and imaginative avenues of the unconscious.

The specialized language of psychoanalysis also proved a hindrance: and the most successful biographies using psychology were those which translated this terminology into literary discourse. I remember that reviewers of my life of Henry James often congratulated me on my not "psychologizing" simply because they could not recognize that I was indeed being very psychological: and it is often the language that turns readers away from the psychoanalytical journals. On the other hand there were writers who borrowed speedily and without knowledge the "Oedipal" of Freud, and it became a trite and meaningless adjective in many articles. Today the new biography can assert, as I have done, that neglect of psychoanalytical psychology means the neglect of a very large area of modern human knowledge. I would go so far as to say that biographies which do not use this knowledge must henceforth be reckoned as incomplete: they belong to a time when lives were entirely "exterior" and neglected the reflective and inner side of human beings.

What biographers need to learn is the basic Freudian knowledge given us about man's ways of thinking, dreaming, and having fantasies. I have told in my book *Stuff of Sleep and Dreams* how I met Freud's dissenting disciple Dr. Alfred Adler in Vienna long ago but I had no occasion in that work to describe my further encounters with psychoanalysis in the 1940s on coming out of the army, and my later testing of transference problems in my biographical writings. From these experiences came some of the innovations in my life of Henry James and the other literary studies and my persistent attempts to translate into common discourse the psychoanalytical terminology to avoid making biographies sound like case histories or therapeutic sessions.

II

Two basic definitions are needed if we are to understand the relevance of psychoanalytic concepts to biography. Psychology deals with the entire field of human behavior; it is an all-inclusive term. Psychoanalysis is the term applied to the special techniques developed by Sigmund Freud and elaborated by his successors for the exploration of the unconscious in therapy. Neither term is altogether satisfactory for our purpose; the term "psychology" is too broad and the term "psychoanalysis" is too narrow. In the psychoanalytic process the analyst has constant access to the unconscious life of the subject—dreams, formulations, slips of the tongue and the pen, associations, the interconnections of experience, rationalization and involuntary memory, the behavior and motivations of daily existence. A biographer also deals in such materials but in a less direct way. They clutter his large table. But how great a difference between having such inert data on the table and having the living subject in a chair or on a couch! A biographer cannot psychoanalyze documents; and yet he searches for the same kind of data as the psychoanalyst—even though he works to different ends. The biographer is not a therapist; and lacks all qualifications for therapy. Dr. Phyllis Greenacre, in her study of Charles Darwin (1963), draws a valuable distinction we may apply here: a distinction between a psychoanalytic writer wishing to write a biography and the psychoanalyst engaged in therapy. She writes:

... the psychoanalytic biographer approaches the study of his subject from vantage points precisely the opposite of those of the psychoanalytic therapist. The latter works largely through the medium of his gradually developing and concentrating relationship with the patient who is seeking help and accepts the relationship for this purpose. The personal involvement and neutrality of the therapist permit the patient to be drawn almost irresistibly into reproducing toward the analyst, in only slightly modified forms, the attitudes (and even their specific content) which have given rise to his difficulties. In this setting, the analyst can help the patient to become feelingly aware of the nature of his difficulties and to achieve a realignment of the conflict-driven forces within him. Psychoanalysis as a *technique* is distinctly for therapeutic purposes and is not generally useful for investigating the personality structure of the individual who is in a good state of balance [pp. 10–11].

This is the very distinction I wish to emphasize. What is the precise difference between the therapeutic analyst working with a living patient and the analytical writer who, so to speak, has to work in a cemetery? Greenacre admirably sums up the kind of work the analytical writer has to do:

He has no direct contact with his subject, and there is no therapeutic aim. He amasses as much material from as many different sources as possible. Lacking the opportunity to study the subject's reactions through the transference neurosis, he must scrupulously scrutinize the situations from which the source material is drawn, and assess the personal interactions involved in it. Further, the study is made for the purpose of extending analytic knowledge and is not sought by the subject [p. 11].

If we accept and learn to understand what "literary psychology" is, we can inject a great deal of clarity in a situation muddled by history—muddled by the term still sometimes used, "applied psychoanalysis." The original belief was that psychoanalysis could be *applied* to literature; but it obviously cannot, for its primary mission is to be applied to a patient. Applied elsewhere it would have to be called nontherapeutic therapy—which is absurd!

To recapitulate: the two essential ingredients of psychoanalysis are the therapist and the patient. But in literary studies we have no patients. We have an unique work by an unique individual. Even if literary folk were qualified, they would be unable to practice psychoanalysis—for there is no psychoanalysis to be practiced. What needs to be more fully recognized is that, in these changed conditions, Freud's *therapeutic* discoveries have little relevance. We take from Freud, however, perhaps the richest part of his work—his insights into man's ways of thinking, dreaming, imagining—those elements that have also an influence on motivations and behavior. It was the good fortune of the world that Sigmund Freud, whose entire focus was on healing, happened to be a great humanist as well. Literature cannot be psychoanalyzed, but it can be analyzed—and this process of analysis, a goodly part of which, as a method, we have derived from Freud, I call literary psychology—the kind of psychology a biographer can use.

III

Biography takes three postulates from psychoanalysis: first, the existence of the unconscious in human motivation and behavior, in dreams, imaginings, thoughts; second, that within the unconscious there exist certain suppressed feelings and states of being which sometimes emerge into awareness in the consciously created forms of literature. When in the form of a dream, these feelings are transformed and disguised material—raw data thrown up by the unconscious, often in mythic and symbolic shape; when in the form of story, poem, play, the same kind of data have been converted by a literary sensibility and temperament, using a vast literary tradition, into a conscious work of art. Third, by the process of induction, that is, by examining the mental representation in words of things not present to the senses, we can discover deeper intentions and meanings, valuable both to the biographer and to the critic. We thus become groping and tentative geographers of the mysterious psyche where fancy is bred. What an enormously difficult task this is! But how mysterious, fascinating and challenging!

No direct ways of proving the existence of the unconscious have been found so far, but to the artist indirect proofs have been available for centuries—and certainly available since Freud showed them to us almost a century ago. Our dreams, our slips of the pen and of the tongue, our whole imagination of being—all give tangible form to things hidden from ourselves. "The artist," said Balzac, that most concrete of novelists, "does not know the secrets of his own mind. ... He does not belong to himself. ... On some days he does not write a line, and if he attempts to, it is not he who holds the pen but his double, his other self. ... And then one evening when he is walking down the street, or one morning when he is getting up, a glowing ember lights his brain." I have quoted Byron, who cut through to the essence of Freud's demonstration of self-delusion. "I feel," said Byron, "that one lies more to one's self than anyone else." Yeats described our reservoirs of drive and conditioning as "an energy as yet uninfluenced by thought, emotion, or action." I like in particular, and have quoted many times, Thoreau's observation that "in dreams we never deceive ourselves, nor are deceived ... in dreams we act a part which we must have learned and rehearsed in our waking hours. ... Our truest life is when we are in the dreams awake." We must not confuse dream magic with what Freud called "preconscious" thought, of which we get abundant proof by our ability to recall, although with some effort, things out of the past. Proust's "involuntary memory"—the madeleine and his cup of lime-flower tea—was an experience of the preconscious. Out of the trigger of taste, he released a chain of remembrances that has been the delight of us all; but behind this remembering there remained Proust's unconscious, living its own life, and driving him for reasons literary psychology must explore, to shut himself in his room as if into the womb of his night to spin his long novel. No criticism or biography of a writer can ever hope to unravel all the marvels of such creative imaginations—all we can hope is to be given a few extraordinary glimpses. And Freud's remark, "Before the problem of the creative artist analysis must, alas, lay down its arms," may be challenged by literary psychology. Before those problems I would say *literary* psychology—in its proper field of the written and spoken word—picks up its arms.

Art is the result not of calm and tranquillity, however much the artist may, on occasion, experience calm in the act of writing. It springs from tension and passion, from a state of disequilibrium in the artist's being. The psychoanalyst, reading the pattern of the work, can attempt to tell us what was wrong with the artist's mental or psychic health. The biographer, reading the same pattern in the larger picture of the human condition, seeks to show how negatives were converted into positives: how Proust translated his allergies and his withdrawal from the pain of experience, into the whole world of Combray, capturing in language the very essences which seemed illusory and evanescent in his consciousness; how Virginia Woolf, on the margin of her melancholy, pinned the feeling of the moment to the printed page as the hunter of butterflies pins his diaphanous and fluttering prize to his; and how James Joyce, visioning himself as Daedalus soaring over a world he had mastered, created a language for it in the word-salads of

Finnegans Wake—but where the schizophrenic patient creates word-salads because of his madness, Joyce created them with that method in madness which Lamb was describing when he spoke of the artist's dominion over his subject. These are the triumphs of art over neurosis, and of literature over life.

In one supreme instance in recent times, the psychoanalyst and the biographer have become one. I refer to Dr. Ernest Jones and the three substantial volumes in which he recorded the life of Sigmund Freud. Dr. Jones wrote out of a deep friendship and a Boswellian knowledge of his subject's life; he wrote also from extensive documents made available to him by the Freud family and as a disciple who had himself arrived at a mastery of psychoanalysis. He ran the inevitable biographical risk of "transference"; but having himself been analyzed he could say at the outset (as he did) that "my own hero-worshipping propensities had been worked through before I encountered [Freud]." Dr. Jones had fewer difficulties in his quest for data than many biographers, although Freud, like Henry James, leveled the approaches to certain areas of his early life by destruction of personal papers. The remaining mass was considerable, however, and more important still, there was available to Dr. Jones in Freud's voluminous writings—the writings of a man with a profound literary sense—much of his subject's self-exploration and his dream life.

The result was a biography of major scope as befitted the luminous mind it celebrated, and a work which uses psychoanalysis constantly while being in itself a partial history of psychoanalysis. *The Life and Work of Sigmund Freud* will probably stand as an archetypal study, illustrating the relation of psychoanalysis to biography—and in negative as well as positive ways. Its shortcomings, for the literary biographer, are fairly obvious: they reside in Dr. Jones's ready use of that language—the concepts, assumptions, conclusions—to which he was accustomed and which had become second nature to him, but which is confusing to the uninitiated reader. The reader without psychoanalytic orientation is asked to make too many leaps and to hurdle ideas that by everyday standards appear strange and inconsistent, and indeed are still open to debate within the psychoanalytic disciplines. One example will suffice. In the first chapter Dr. Jones describes the emotional problems which beset the two-year-old Freud upon the impending birth of another child in the family:

> Darker problems arose when it dawned on him that some man was even more intimate with his mother than he was. Before he was two years old, for the second time another baby was on the way, and soon visibly so. Jealousy of the intruder, and anger for whoever had seduced his mother into such an unfaithful proceeding, were inevitable. Discarding his knowledge of the sleeping conditions in the house, he rejected the unbearable thought that the nefarious person could be his beloved and perfect father.

Dr. Jones here imputes the insights of a full-fledged analyst to a two-year-old. This is a curious slip, endowing a baby—even a baby destined to become the founder of psychoanalysis—with more precocity than it had at the time. I think it illustrates the biographer's failure to instruct the reader in the differences between the unconscious and conscious life we all lead.

One needs to be more than merely conversant with Freudian theory to grasp this picture of a childish consciousness told in the terms of adult sexuality. Dr. Jones was inevitably much less concerned with the *translation* of his specialized concepts into the language of everyday life. The literary biographer, when he borrows the psychoanalyst's code, is obliged to decipher it and render it into language proper to literature and to the prose narrative on which he is engaged.

IV

We have for decades used general psychological concepts in criticism and biography without question. When we discuss the motivations of Hamlet, is not this psychology? When we try to understand and speculate upon symbols in a poem, are we not "psychologizing"? And in our time, when creative writers have been exposed directly to the works of Freud and Jung and their disciples, and use them in their writings, we must treat them for the sources that they are. How can we understand William Faulkner's *Light in August* without a glance at certain modern theories of "conditioning" and behavior? Can we deal adequately with *Finnegans Wake* without looking into Jung and his theory of the collective unconscious? The answer to the misguided use of psychoanalysis is not to close our ears, but to ask ourselves: how are we to handle this difficult material while remaining true to our own disciplines—and avoid making complete fools of ourselves?

It is fairly obvious that we can handle it only after we have studied and mastered that part of psychology useful to us, as we must master any learning. Our success will depend entirely on the extent to which we know what we are about and the way in which we learn to use this new and intricate code. Critics who babble of the Oedipus complex and who plant psychoanalytical clichés

higgledy-piggledy in their writing do a disservice both
to literature and to psychoanalysis.

We come then to the logical question which follows
all that I have said. How are critics and biographers to
obtain the specialized training that might give them
greater awareness of man's unconscious, and greater
insight into the ways of the human imagination? Psychoanalysis is a therapy, and not a training school—
although most analysts undergo analysis to discover their
own hang-ups and to avoid getting these mixed up with
their patients. Moreover, it is too arduous and too costly
and not necessarily indicated. We know from Edwin
Muir's autobiography that he was analyzed and that this
occurred because an analyst became interested in him;
and that in the process he discovered he could write poetry.
But his was also a difficult case for the analysis seemed
to break certain of his defences and impelled him toward
a nightmare world. The analysis was quite properly ter-
minated. Analytic institutes offer special courses for
individuals in nonpsychiatric disciplines, and we know
how much the awareness of unconscious modes has
influenced religious studies, myth studies, anthropology,
linguistics, history and so many other disciplines. Of late,
however, there have been experiments which might prove
helpful to those of us engaged in literary studies. I am
thinking of a paper by Dr. George Moraitis of the Chicago Institute of Psychoanalysis, "A Psychoanalyst's
Journey into a Historian's World: An Experiment in
Collaboration." By "collaboration" he does not mean that
he took any part in the historian's job of work—in this
particular case a study of Nietzsche. His role was to illuminate the approach to the job, the historian's attitudes
and ideas, and to be a consultant or advisor. The collaboration was a continuous dialogue, in which the histo-

rian Dr. Carl Pletsch spoke out of his expertise and Dr. Moraitis out of his analytical training. No therapy was involved. Another analyst was used as consultant. He went over the data and helped clarify any confusions that might have arisen in this interpersonal encounter of analyst and researcher. Dr. Moraitis at all times called himself the guest of the historian; the historian in turn was the host of the analyst. In this way the nontherapeutic relationship was further emphasized.

The historian showed signs of resistance from the first. He proposed at the initial encounter that instead of working on Nietzsche they work on Bismarck. Moraitis explored this resistance promptly. Why did the historian, who had spent so much time on Nietzsche and was writing a study, attempt to turn to a wholly fresh subject? Several things were revealed—the historian's fear that his private preserve in Nietzsche might be trespassed upon; his curious sense of proprietorship. There was evidence in this also of his emotional involvement with Nietzsche. But the analyst noticed other symptoms: the historian's negative tone, his choice of words, his intensities—even while he announced that his feelings toward Nietzsche were entirely neutral. By this direct kind of exploration of the work-situation, and Dr. Moraitis's insistence that their task was to explore Nietzsche's personality not the investigator's, the historian loosened up considerably. What was being explored in these encounters, in reality long talk-sessions (in which the analyst came thoroughly briefed by heavy homework in Nietzsche), was to find the boundaries of the task and the psychological forces that influenced it.

This experiment yielded other evidence. At one point the analyst developed his own "object transference" toward Nietzsche and for a while he had to discuss with the disinterested consultant whether he could maintain his own analytical neutrality. This made him speculate whether the pooling of work of several investigators might not help to further understand "the varied transference reactions" of each investigator. What emerged was a strange reversal of position. The historian became increasingly interested in Nietzsche's life, whereas the analyst saw in this a further resistance to dealing with Nietzsche's work—a resistance "to the appreciation of Nietzsche's intellectual work and possibly even an effort to demean him." Moraitis, having himself became involved with the life and work of Nietzsche while studying the historian's reactions, found himself pondering whether "the creativity of one individual can only be mastered through the creativity of another." He came to the conclusion that the historian was attempting to see Moraitis "as Nietzsche and to test his insights on me. In this situation, the reader position was actually a Nietzsche position, which impelled the historian to identify me as the ideal reader." The historian's negative feelings toward Nietzsche then were transferred into positive feelings toward the analyst who was absorbing and using Nietzsche's writings and was taking attitudes that now seemed to the historian to be favorable to Nietzsche. There seemed in this to be a double transference, or a transference toward Nietzsche of a more positive kind through the agency of analyst-approval of the subject.

I will not go further into this rich paper but I want to stress the possibilities that it opens up—the kind of consultation that might be made possible if other psychoanalysts were willing to pursue the multiple problems involved in biographical and historical "transference." A great many loose threads remain and probably always will remain. Moraitis recognized that the predicament of the historian was more difficult than his own. He remained firmly on the ground of his professional observations and analysis: the historian was called upon to meet difficult demands. These could be assumed, said Moraitis, only "by individuals with a deep sense of conviction and trust." The historian was encouraged to involve himself in examination of his own motivations and emotions and to purge himself of certain resistances and angers he had developed toward his subject and his work. Such consultations, properly planned, can enable researchers to avoid gratuitous surmise. They would be of little use to biographers addicted wholly to externals and concretions—biographers unable to seek for inner things. But the subjective biographer needs to be protected from his own subjectivity; needs to be able to stand back and observe himself in the act of rationalization and self-deception. There are critics and biographers who are too easily satisfied with their extrapolations and conclusions and are unwilling to see that there exist always depths within depths, and that we are the prey as well as the beneficiary of our own fantasies. By consultation of qualified help, the burden of inquiry can be lightened, and insights hitherto blocked by subjective resistances can be removed. Whenever a biographer or critic searches deeply enough into himself or herself there is less danger of oversimplified answers to highly complicated states of being. Few critics have been able to resist making their texts a part of their own mind and feeling; or their own drive to power. Often there has been a great deal of posturing in the mirrors of the self. And very few biographers can be said to have conquered their emotional involvements with their materials. In this I am mindful, in our recent attention to the lives of women written by feminists, of such gross exaggerations as occur, for

Myth

A PORTRAIT GALLERY—a national portrait gallery—evokes great pages of history, the distant and the near past. It is an exhilarating experience to come upon faces of characters one has known only in history books. I remember a particular thrill of my youth when I wandered into the rooms of Britain's National Portrait Gallery housing the eminent Victorians—so eminent, so assured, so rubicund, so gouty, so marked in feature and countenance. I was at large in the nineteenth century with Spencer and Huxley, Darwin and Green, Gladstone and Disraeli. Equally thrilling was the experience of finding myself among writers all the way back to the romantics—Byron, sexy and sultry in his Eastern turban; Shelley, looking startled; Coleridge, broad and large as life; the Brontës on a primitive canvas painted by their brother, the canvas by which we alone know them. There is a fascinating relationship between the painter or sculptor who, with his plastic resources, gives us the visual appearance of a life and a personality, and the biographer who traces these features in an essay or book. It is fairly obvious that a painted portrait or a chiseled bust cannot be a total biography. But at its best, when the bust or the portrait comes from the hand of a master, it is certainly more than a mask, it is an essence of a life, usually a great life, and it captures—when painterly eyes and shaping hands have looked and seized it—certain individual traits and features, and preserves them for posterity, for that life beyond life, of which Milton so eloquently spoke. Biography seeks to arrive at similar essences. I speak inevitably of the large figures, of endowed renderings. We need not concern ourselves with "camp" biographies or daubs, the ephemeral figures of movie stars, dope addicts, Boston stranglers; they belong to certain kinds of life histories written by journalists in our time. They belong in a waxworks. They are documentary and often vividly mythic; they are more related to the photographic, the visual moment, the changing world of entertainment or crime, the great and flourishing field of interminable gossip disseminated by the media. This is quite distinct, as we know, from serious artistic biographical and pictorial quests to capture the depths and mysteries of singular greatness.

I

The painter paints what he sees—and sometimes *sees into*—when he offers us a portrait from life. The biographer is governed by greater complexities than plasticity, color, canvas. What rationale governs the scope, the shape, the perception of a given life that is to be expressed in words? By what general principles does the biographer finally put together his portrait, his documented biography? I would suggest that when we look at those living walls of the national portrait galleries we are seeing largely the individuals as they were in process of living out their mythic lives, acclaimed or neglected, struggling or showing triumph—or defeat. The proud carriage of Byron, the startled look of Shelley, the young Brontës fixed in their untested youth by their brother's amateur brush, all these give us a considerable measure of external aspects, appearances, stance. We must consider two kinds of myth: the myth we perceive with our eyes and sense of observation; and the covert myth, which is a part of the hidden dreams of our biographical subjects, and which even they would have difficulty to describe because these are lodged in the unconscious, in the psyche.

The covert myth has to be deduced from the public myth, and from the stray bits of psychological evidence offered us by our subjects, the little hints, the casual remarks, or the poetry or prose set down out of themselves.

The method I am proposing for biography is related to the methods of Sherlock Holmes and also to those of Sigmund Freud. If one approaches an archive with the right questions, one carries a series of important keys to locked doors. The right doors will open if the right questions are asked; the mountains of trivia will melt away, and essences will emerge. Many historians have unconsciously worked in this way, but I am not aware that we have consciously sought to describe a *method*. This is not easy, nor can this method be mechanically learned. It requires a certain kind of talent, a certain kind of inwardness to look at the reverse of a tapestry, to know when and where to seek the figure under the carpet. Our concern is how to deal with this clutter, how to confront our subject, how to achieve the clean mastery of the portrait painter not often concerned with archives, who reads only the lines in the face, the settled mouth, the color of the cheeks, the brush strokes and pencil marks of time. More often than not this offers us the revealing mask of life. The biographer must learn to know the mask—and in doing this he will have won half the battle. The other half is his real battle, the most difficult part of his task—his search for what I call the figure under the carpet, the evidence on the reverse of the tapestry, the life-myth of a given mask. In an archive, we wade simply and securely through paper and photocopies and related concrete materials. But in our quest for the life-myth we tread on dangerous speculative and inferential ground, ground that requires all of our attention, all of our accumulated resources. For we must read certain psychological signs that enable us to understand what people are really saying behind the faces they put on, behind the utterances they allow themselves to make before the world.

II

What do I mean by the hidden personal myth? Let me take a writer like Ernest Hemingway, whose life and habits have been widely recorded, not least by a circle of his relatives and friends. We know he liked to shoot, to fish, to drink; we know that he was boastful. He wanted to be champion. He wanted to fight wars—on his own terms—and shoot big game and catch the biggest fish and live the manliest life—the super-man life. Was not one of his books entitled *Men Without Women?* That tells us something—though it may not be what you think. Small wonder that Max Eastman asked a very proper biographical question—why did Hemingway make such a fuss about the hair on his chest? And we remember that when Hemingway ran into Eastman in Maxwell Perkins's office at Scribner's, he proved Eastman's insight by demanding a fight. The two writers ended on the floor with a great flailing of arms and legs. "I wasn't going to box with him," Eastman said when he described the incident to me. "I just put my arms around him and embraced him." Hemingway wanted to prove he had hair on his chest. Now the obvious myth—and I choose Hemingway because he can be read so easily—was the novelist's drive to do the biggest, kill the biggest, achieve the greatest, and that is written large in all his books. A code of drive and courage, simple, direct, masculine, excessively masculine; and a code in the art of trying to shape and simplify and crystallize and not get too close to feeling. That is the manifest myth. But as a biographer, I go beyond this and ask—what does Hemingway express? What is Hemingway saying to us in all his books and all his actions? A great deal, and as is nearly always the case, much that is exactly the opposite of what he seems to be saying. A manly man doesn't need to prove his masculinity every moment of the day. Only someone who is troubled and not at all secure with himself and with his role puts up his fists and spoils for a fight over a casual remark by an easygoing and affectionate person like Max Eastman. The biographical questions multiply, and in effect we ask ourselves: What is Hemingway defending himself against, so compulsive is his drive toward action and away from examined feeling, so consistent is his quest to surpass himself, as if he always must prove—even after he has had the world's acclaim—that he is the best and the greatest. Critics have remarked on this, and I say nothing that has not already been widely discussed—but it illustrates what I mean by the figure under the carpet. Hemingway's figure *in* the carpet is his pattern of seeking out violence wherever he can find it, seeking out courage, resignation, heroism and perseverance, and avoiding too much feeling. But the reverse of the tapestry tells us that somewhere within resides a troubled, uncertain, insecure figure, who works terribly hard to give himself eternal assurance. Where there seems to be immense fulfillment, we discern extraordinary inadequacy—and self-flagellation and a high competitiveness; also, a singular want of generosity toward his fellow artists, since he must always proclaim himself the champ. Life reduced to the terms of the bullring and the prize fight is a very narrow kind of life indeed. The biography of Hemingway that captures the real portrait, the portrait within, still needs to be written. And what is important in Hemingway's archive, which is large, are the answers to the questions that will relate his doubts, his failures, his struggles, and not the answers to his successes that are written in the public prints.

I will now take an example less obvious and less well known—that of Henry David Thoreau. The biographers of Thoreau have always accepted his view of himself and his mission at Walden Pond "to suck the marrow of life," that is, to meditate and learn the virtues of simplicity and solitude, and not be a slave to the bondages of life, like mortgages and banks and the humdrum entanglements of the farmer, for whom Thoreau expresses considerable contempt. *Walden* is a beautiful book, an exquisite distillation of the intentions and desires of Thoreau, a work of the imagination that pretends it is a true story, and it embodies a myth that all America—indeed the whole world—has adopted: that of getting away from the slavery of civilization, facing the world as God made it, not as man ravaged it. This is one part of Thoreau's story, and it is a part of his greatness. The question a biographer seeking the truth must equally ask if he wants to see the figure under Thoreau's carpet is, what motivated him to this idealistic undertaking?

Why did he decide to built a hut? In other words, why beyond his own beautiful rationalizations—did he *really* go to Walden pond? That seems to be a difficult question to answer. Yet by focusing on it within the materials of Thoreau's life a number of answers emerge. There is that day the remarkable woodsman went fishing and in cooking the fish set fire to the woods and almost burned Concord down. There is the simple fact that the farmers had quite as much contempt for Thoreau as he had for them. There is the evidence that Concord thought him a man of enormous talent who idled his time away walking in the woods. There is the man who said he'd rather shake the outstretched branch of a tree than the hand of Henry Thoreau. And there is Emerson who quoted this over Thoreau's grave. Thoreau's hut, we learn, did not stand in great loneliness; he did not plant it in a wilderness. He planted it on Emerson's land on the shores of Walden with Emerson's consent. This made it easy for him to criticize those who had to pay rent or mortgages. The railway lay within easy distance. His mother's house was one mile down the road and, said the Boston hostess, Annie Fields, in her diary, David Thoreau was a *very* good son, "even when living in his retirement at Walden Pond, he would come home every day." Others have told us that he raided the family cookie jar while describing how he subsisted on the beans he grew in his field. To discover this, and to remember how often Thoreau dined with the Emersons, and gregariously joined the citizens of Concord around the crackerbarrel in the local store, is to overlook his life struggle, the inner biographical problem that the literary portrait painter must face. The evidence can be read in the moving parable within the pages of *Walden,* which tells us more than a thousand letters might in an archive. Thoreau wrote: "I long ago lost a hound, a bay horse, and a turtle dove, and am still on their trail. Many are the travellers I have spoken concerning them, describing their tracks and what calls they answer to. I have met one or two who had heard the hound, and the tramp of the horse, and even seen the dove disappear behind a cloud, and they seemed as anxious to recover them as if they had lost them themselves."

Loss and anxiety about loss—a bay horse, a hound, a turtle dove. Thoreau's little parable, which he launches enigmatically in *Walden,* contains a great deal that a biographer needs to guide him into the reverse of the tapestry of the author of *Walden.* Here, in capsule, are the three members of the animal kingdom closest to mankind: the faithful hound, guide, protector, loving and lovable; the horse of Thoreau's time, plower of fields, the embodiment of strength, thrust and support, and the spirited symbol of all that is instinctual in man; and finally the turtle dove, the soft cooing swift messenger, bearer of tidings as in the Bible, symbol of love and of the Holy Ghost. The biographer of Thoreau must write not the story of a solitude-loving, nature-loving, eternally quest-ing self-satisfied isolate who despises his neighbors, and is despised by them, but the story of a man who feels he has lost the deepest parts of himself—without guide and support, without strength and love, a lost little boy of Concord, a loner, a New England narcissus. The biog-raphy would have to be written not in a debunking spirit but in compassion and with the realization that this man who felt he had lost so much was able to transcend his losses and create an American myth and the work of art known as *Walden.*

166]

III

"Men of genius never can explain their genius," said Henry James in writing to a famous British soldier. Balzac explained his genius by using a Greek myth. "As between Faust and Prometheus," he said, "I would choose Prometheus." His choice of the great god-benefactor of the Greeks, the giver of fire, the teacher of the useful arts, is characteristic of Balzac who was a great "giver"— a writer who ceaselessly poured out the plenitude of his genius. His choice measures for us with precision his self-concept. The Promethean myth is all action, passion and creation. But Prometheus was also punished for his affront of the gods. He was chained to a rock—as Balzac symbolically chained himself to his armchair and wrote for eighteen hours a day (and night) so that he might produce several novels a year. Prometheus's liver was gnawed by an eagle in daylight, but restored during the night for further gnawing—very like Balzac, the prodigal spender who constantly created new debts to pay off his old debts, which meant that he was a chronic borrower, gnawed by his debts.

A reader of Balzac's life encounters Balzac's father, who with a group of friends created a *tontine*—a gamble in which these men paid annuities to their own little insurance company, survivor take all. Balzac turned this topsy-turvy into a remarkable early novel called *La Peau de Chagrin*—a tale of a wild ass's skin which his hero acquires in a fantastic and mysterious curiosity shop. The possessor of the skin discovers he can fulfill any wish— but for a price; with each wish the skin shrinks. When the entire skin is gone he will die. The skin is the symbol of our shrinking days. Balzac, lifting his tale out of the

Arabian Nights, read it into post-Napoleonic Paris. His father had paid his subscriptions into a gamble that he would outlive the others; he had lived for a problematical future that never arrived, for he died before some of the others. Balzac lived for the present and paid with his life for his long-planned future. In his case it was win first, then lose all, as in the *Peau de Chagrin.* Like Prometheus, the French novelist was the slave of his passions and his appetites, and the slave of his debts. He had to keep writing. "To be forever creating!" he exclaimed. "Even God created for only six days." His devoted friend Madame Carraud asked: "When shall I see you work for the sake of work?" Obsessed by his dream of fame, fortune and Napoleonic power, ridden by his demons, Balzac drove himself beyond any novelist in the history of fiction. He turned night into day, fortified by torrents of coffee. Beginning at midnight, he wrote for hours at a stretch, slept six hours, and started all over again, and kept this pace for weeks on end. He paid his price. He died at fifty-one, worn out by his prodigious effort. But he brought into being his *Comédie Humaine,* even though he left it unfinished. Maurois put Balzac's central dilemma in an aphorism: "A man whose greatest malady was his genius."

The life of Balzac is the history of that malady, the story of how Balzac burned his shrinking candle—with the brightest flame—at both ends. When one looks at the shelves he filled, the scenes he visited, the women he loved, the contemporaries he touched, the extravagant illusions he turned into realities, one recognizes the power of his creativity and the large interwoven world which found issue in his books. To be sure, many of his tales have dated; his audience of women (especially those over thirty who still had a hope of love) would probably not respond as profoundly to certain of his books today. But in his total work, his picture of the empire's *arriviste* world, he wove a Breughel-like fictional tapestry. Money and power, these were his subjects. What he did not know he imagined. What he imagined acquired a sense of truth because of his feverish belief in it. He knew how to draw men and women in their environment, and to show this environment working through them as their destiny.

We might add that he achieved his work by his extraordinary sense of life's concretions; yet he was also a visionary. With his gambler's appetite, his prolonged love affair with the Countess Hanska, his friendship with Hugo, Sand, Gautier, and his eternal sense of *gloire*, he believed that fame and success would justify all his pretensions, all his fables. One critic said that "everything he wrote was but the preface to what he meant to write," and we might add his life was a constant preparation for the life he wanted to live.

Balzac finally married his countess, purchased his great house in Paris, filled it with antiques, attained the life style of the aristocrat he had dreamed and redreamed in his novels—but it was too late. He was dying of his fulfilled dreams. All had been accomplished except the duration of his life to enjoy his spoils. Victor Hugo came to see the dying novelist in that great house; amid the antiques and bric-à-brac he saw the animator lifeless on his deathbed, and, reaching under the coverlet, grasped in farewell the hand of genius, a hand already growing limp. Balzac's face was purple, almost black; his hair was cut short and was gray, and his eye was open and fixed. "I saw his face in profile and he resembled the emperor," Hugo wrote. The emperor too had gambled on the grand scale and died before his time. Balzac's covert myth had been an imperial myth—the myth of his father that the winner would take all. He did everything by a tremendous effort of the will, and his myth engulfed him and killed him.

IV

I have often wondered how a life-myth is connected sometimes with the name bestowed so often light-heartedly by parents on their progeny. For example, Ralph Ellison, the author of *Invisible Man,* that striking mythic parable of our time, may have been destined for literature by his parents who combined the name Ellison with that of Emerson and named their son Ralph Waldo. When certain children, possessed of a strong will and drive, bear a proud name, they acquire a sense of their own significance; the name carries an emanation of grandeur or greatness; represents on occasion a kind of consecration and gives a sense of vocation, purpose, status, responsibility. We find a striking example in the name of Martin Luther King, who was originally named Michael but later renamed by his clergyman father and given the name of the father of Protestantism. Small wonder that he felt he should, as it were, nail his thesis to the church door and say *Ich kann nicht anders.* He was no longer a Protestant only in name; there was sufficient matter for a great protest. If that seems to describe his public myth he often, in his sermons and speeches, enunciated another myth linked to his kingly name. He was Martin Luther; he was also an Old Testament king who never ruled—he was Moses who led his people out of slavery into the Promised Land. Martin Luther King fulfilled in his abbreviated life all that his name implied.

Rex Stout, the author of widely read detective novels, was given his name of Rex by his mother on the day of his birth "because he came out like a king." When Stout named his detective he chose a name of an evil emperor— a promotion from rex to *imperator,* and called him Nero Wolfe. But he turned him into a worker against evil. The Wolfe hearked back to a family name, that of Todhunter, hunter of foxes. In changing his kingly name to emperor, and fox into wolf Rex Stout baptized his character in personal ironies and personal mythology— the recall of the bad emperor had a good purpose, the hunting of criminals. The choice of the name, the trans-positions made, tells us a great deal of the life-stance of this imaginative and entertaining writer.

The names of Martin Luther King and of Rex Stout remind me of the case of another King who became prime minister of Canada and remained in office for three decades. William Lyon Mackenzie King was a portly man with heavy features, and dignity of bearing. He was a compromiser in politics, a political tactician. He man-aged to steer his country through the crises of this cen-tury by a kind of renewable stasis. His case has much interest for biography, and a perceptive life remains to be written. He was descended from William Lyon Mackenzie, one of the founders of Canada's political sys-tem. To be christened with an ancestral political name and to possess the family name of King seemed a sum-mons to leadership. In school his fellow-students nick-named him Rex. The sense of self is never stronger than when it carries a meaningful designation: there is no need to wonder who they are, or what purpose they must have. Mackenzie King impressed early by his compe-tence and leadership. He learned administration in the United States as a "foundation executive." At the right moment he moved into Canadian political life and into the world scene as if this had been preordained.

The name in the Canadian case so useful, mythically, for public life, proved inadequate for the prime minister's private life. He kept careful diaries of his personal thoughts and actions and these show how his kingship became a mask of desolation. Public success turned to ashes once the prime minister was face to face with himself. His diaries reveal an abject loneliness, an inability to acquire the friendship and crowded personal life that most often accompanies a high position. The reticences and puritanism of his upbringing had given him no awareness of how to conduct himself with women; and an attachment to his mother had deprived him of all sense of other women. He was a success in national politics, a failure in sexual politics. In his case, status-ego and political-ego rigidified his inability to unbend—to take a woman in his arms, to kiss her, to show some sign of love or affection. In his youth he had resorted to brothels; but these filled him with so much guilt that he got no pleasure from them. His political power was devoid of sexual power.

This emerges in the diaries. King's biographer, Colonel C.P. Stacey, perhaps because he is primarily a military historian, sees only the oddity of King's behavior without understanding its roots or recognizing the waste and pathos of his peculiar situation. The wives of public men took pity on King and helped him as hostesses or mother figures, and for a time he found one companion who looked after some of the formal functions in his life. But always at the end of the day there remained for William Lyon Mackenzie King the lonely bed, the self-communion of his diary and emotional emptiness. It was a case of public fulfillment and private failure.

The height of this curious drama was reached when King, in effect emotionally dead, developed a cult of the dead. He took up spiritualism. He cultivated mediums. He held seances, trying to commune with the ghosts of his unlived life. It wasn't the sort of thing a man in public office was supposed to do, and it was on the whole a well-kept secret. The death of the soul had occurred early. Since this loneliest of men could not communicate with the living outside officialdom and public service, he sought to talk to the dead. This is the biographical story that emerged from the diaries—a drama of the psyche with tragic overtones, however much some want to see it as having a comic side.

I am not suggesting that everyone with a significant name out of history or the past necessarily aspires to live up to that name. But there are certain instances where the name becomes a part of the symbolic life, and is encased in a private myth. There must exist certain drives and certain kinds of selfhood to the enhancement of name and character. It would be scientifically interesting to take a sampling of individuals with particular and unusual names and explore their fantasies derived from their psychological role-playing. No biography can be effective if the subject's self-concept is not studied: the private myth provides a covert drive and motivating force.

[173

Narratives

FORM

THERE COMES A MOMENT when the biographer must call a halt. The pursuit of his helpless subject cannot continue forever. The clutter on the worktable must be put into some order. Seated behind his materials, the biographer must collect his wits and start to write. At this moment, with blank sheets of paper before him, the literary investigator, the critic, the psychologist become one—the biographer.

It can be an awful moment. Where begin? How in that welter of material amid the multitudinous months and days of another's life, is he to find those points of departure which will enable him to proceed? In his mind a million facts exert simultaneous pressure; around him are notes and files which now must be converted into a readable book; and all this crowded detail must flow in an orderly fashion and in lucid prose, must be fitted into a narrative, calm and measured and judicial, capable of capturing a reader and conveying in some degree the intensity which has kept the biographer for long months at his task.

What kind of biography shall it be? How much of the material can be used? And in what manner is the story to be told? Biographers do not consciously sit down at the last moment to ask themselves these questions; the questions have been asked before, while they have labored: the answers, however, must be found in the final act of writing. At some point the decision has had to be taken which will determine the scope of the work and the technique of narration. To some extent the importance of the life that is being written may dictate an answer, and the writing, also, will be profoundly influenced by the quantity and nature of the materials. Thus a commemorative biography or an authorized biography will, by its nature, tend to be seen quite differently from a biography written as a result of the biographer's own deep interest in the subject.

There are, in biography, as many kinds of garments as there are subjects to wear them, and each garment will have its special cut and its particular frills and decorations. It is not my intention here to imitate Carlyle and to offer a disquisition upon biographical dress. In the opening pages of *Sartor Resartus* the author observes that "neither in tailoring nor in legislating does man proceed by mere Accident, but the hand is ever guided on by mysterious operations of the mind. In all his Modes, and habilitory endeavours, an Architectural Idea will be found lurking." I think at least three main Architectural Ideas can be found in the structure of biographies. The first and most common is the traditional documentary biography, an integrated work in which the biographer arranges the materials—Boswell did this—so as to allow the voice of the subject to be heard constantly (even when that voice is heard in converse with his own biographer, as in the case of Boswell). The second type of biography is the creation, in words, of something akin to the painter's portrait. Here the picture is somewhat more circumscribed; it is carefully sketched in, and a frame is placed around it. The third type, which has been fashioned less often in our time, is one in which the materials are melted down and in which the biographer is present in the work as omniscient narrator. We are given largely, in such a work, the biographer's vision of his subject. The first type of biography might be said to be chronicle; the second pictorial; the third narrative-pictorial or "novelistic."

The chronicle life is a large, roomy life in which documents are constantly in the foreground, and the author is never so happy as when quoting liberally from them. Often such works are "official biographies," that is, works designed as standard lives "for the record," and in the circumstance the biographer is inclined, and indeed obliged, to put into the book a great deal more than would be used by other biographers. In a portrait biography, a principle of high selectivity is inherent in the form; though the portrait-biographers more often than not lean heavily upon official lives, they might be said to represent the entire landscape around a portion of which the frame will be placed. For the chronicle life essential background is established; documents are usually presented in chronological fashion and annotated. Sometimes the background looms very large. Masson's life of Milton is a good example of a "life and times" treatment validly employed in one of the large-dimensioned biographies of our literature, because Milton's life touched its time at so many points. The result is a work of history created around a central figure—and since letters and private papers are given *in extenso,* a heavy autobiographical component is introduced into the biographical creation. Documents, however, are seldom all-revealing. There remains something inevitably arbitrary about the chronicle procedure. It is arbitrary because some letters are preserved through fortuitous circumstances and others disappear. Who is to know whether those preserved are not sometimes the trivial, and those which have disappeared the important? In such a biography no particular attempt is made, usually, to rehearse any portion of the life in dramatic form; if the biographer writing in this fashion has a large sense of life, and is accomplished in the art of expression, he can endow the work with a certain amount of grandeur by the sense of continuity and completeness, weight and authority it conveys—for all its inherent incompleteness. The figure is there, and sometimes it lives because the documents themselves are alive and impart to the orderly text a constant vividness; and sometimes also because the entire structure breathes the vitality and informing mind of the biographer as well. The combination of vivid subject and vivid biographer, however, is rare; more often than not vividness goes a-begging in the hands of pedestrian but meticulous biographers who, when they have finished, have merely placed the reader in front of their well-arranged worktable. Or, to vary the image, they leave on our hands a frozen statue, cold as marble, and as sepulchral.

The second biographical type frankly calls itself a "portrait." When it is actually written as one, not merely so named, it is something quite different from the classical chronicle type of biography. It derives in a sense from those minutes of lives which John Aubrey recorded in the seventeenth century; it is the biography of an individual in brief; it seeks to catch the essential traits, all that will characterize and express the personality and suggest the life *behind* the surface exhibited to the world; it employs a minimum of background, and, as in the painting of a portrait, frames the subject in a given position. The English Men of Letters series, that splendid though unequal group of literary biographies first edited by John Morley, contained a number of well-told lives which, in their concision and adherence to subject alone, might be considered as "portraits." And there is that hybrid, also a kind of portrait, which bears the title *critical biography:* that is, a biography which seeks to delineate the subject in terms of the works and by a critical discussion of these is able to convey some picture of the creating mind or personality. In my opinion, however, such portraits are matters of accident, or approximations of the pictorial life.

The very type and model of the portrait biography in our time, it seems to me, is Geoffrey Scott's *The Portrait of Zélide.* It is a work compounded of grace and charm; it is written with a rare economy of word and phrase, almost as if each were a brush stroke; the style is inimitable, as good styles are. The portrait is of a vigorous lady of the rational century who scribbled novels at Neuchâtel and whose path was crossed briefly by the peripatetic Boswell and, for a longer period, by a mercurial gentleman who bore the unmercurial name of Constant. If we examine the strokes by which Geoffrey Scott (he was an architect turned man of letters) painted his portrait of Zélide, or, as history better knows her, Madame de Charrière, we see that he had but few documents to draw upon: some bundles of letters, preserved by accident (including a long, fatuous, and extremely droll missive from Boswell); a weighty chronicle life, written by a Neuchâtel professor, essentially archival in character; and the writings of Benjamin Constant and of Madame de Charrière herself. Yet so carefully did Scott read himself into this distant time that Zélide is there before us, all verve and quick intelligence in action or in repose: first as she was in that old house at Zuylen, in Holland, where she was born and "from whose walls innumerable Van Tuylls looked down in stiff disapproval of their too lively descendant," and later in Utrecht or in Paris or in the sleepy manor at Neuchâtel where she, who had scorned the dullness of Holland, finally settled for that long, dull married life her mind willed her into, against the better dictates of her heart. "Madame de Charrière," wrote Geoffrey Scott at the beginning of his biographical portrait,

> was not of marble, emphatically, nor even of the hardness of Houdon's clay. But the coldness of Houdon's bust—its touch of aloofness—corresponds to an intellectual ideal, more masculine than feminine, which she set before herself. It embodies a certain harsh clear cult of the reason which at every crisis falsified her life. She was not more reasonable, in the last resort, than the rest of humanity. She paid in full and stoically, the penalty of supposing herself to be so.

The clarity with which Scott sees his characters, placing each in its limited scene, and his capacity—rare among writers and scholars—for reading the emotions in his documents as well as the words, enables him to trace for us with a pen lyrical and psychological the course of two obsessions: Benjamin Constant's and Madame de Charrière's for each other:

> The attraction was between two minds, bewilderingly akin. To each the self-conscious analysis of every pulse and instant of life, of every problem and situation, was as necessary as a vice. Benjamin was a libertine when the mood was on him, just as in other moods he became an ambitious author or a politician; but he was a thinker always; and his intellect never worked with more startling clearness than when his emotions were involved. The thing he shared with

Madame de Charrière—this rapid clarity and ceaseless gymnastic of the mind—was not a mood, but the man himself. Understanding that, holding him by that, she held him as strongly as any woman could.

And Geoffrey Scott is led to the question that all his readers would inevitably ask. Were they then lovers, these two minds? "The subject has its pedantries like any other," Scott writes, "I will not explore them," and he thus foregoes the opportunity for the kind of speculation which certain biographers, (Maurois for example) would relish. "Psychologically," Geoffrey Scott adds, "the character of their relation is abundantly clear; technically the inquiry would be inconclusive."

Biography is never finer than when it is as candid as this. To the quick sketch which Geoffrey Scott draws in the early pages of his work, the portrait itself remains loyal, so that we have at the end the expected culminating point. Belle de Zuylen, Madame de Charrière, awaits death "a frond of flame; a frond of frost." It is tempting to linger with the quiet wit, and the crisp, almost metallic style, as eighteenth-century as its subject, by which Geoffrey Scott brought to life this woman long dead, and engaged our interest in her. But we must pass on to further definitions.

I would invoke, however, one more example of a portrait, painted during the 1940s, which, perhaps because of this, has not received the attention it deserves: Percy Lubbock's *Portrait of Edith Wharton*. It is a portrait drawn with the same concision as that of Zélide, but it is derived from more ample materials; also this time the biographer had known his subject. Lubbock's method, no less urbane and suave than his predecessor's, was to assemble the testimony of Edith Wharton's friends, early and late.

We see Mrs. Wharton through a series of "points of view"—a not unexpected device on the part of the author of *The Craft of Fiction*. What these two portraits have in common is their essentially two-dimensional quality, their constant focusing on the central figure. To create a good biographical portrait requires the greatest kind of economy, a constant sensitivity to the materials (or shall we say pigments?), and an eye for all that characterizes and "represents," all that is vivid and human in the subject.

The third type of biography is at once larger than the portrait and yet smaller than the full-length biography. In this kind of biography the documents are seldom quoted at length, but are melted down and refined so that a figure may emerge, a figure in immediate action and against changing backgrounds. Such a work tends to borrow from the methods of the novelist without, however, becoming fiction. Here biography is not concerned with strict chronology; it may shuttle backward and forward in a given life and seek to disengage scenes or utilize trivial incidents—which others might discard—to illuminate character. The biographer is so saturated with documents as to be free from their bondage. By means wholly selective and psychological, some truth may be reached.

Lytton Strachey was the father of this kind of biography in our time. He is now under eclipse, and I fear that many of his gifts of style and of insight, as well as his biographical innovations, are overlooked because he allowed his hostility to the Victorians to color much of his work. His animus pervades *Eminent Victorians;* the very title is tinged with irony once we discover what Strachey does to their eminence. And while his biography of Queen Victoria is written with a mellower pen, we are never in doubt that he disapproved of what might be called the Queen's "middle-classiness," her rigidities, her sentimentality, her aesthetic blindnesses, those very qualities by which he shows her human and fallible—although a queen. Strachey was a master of biographical irony. Irony, however, can distort as well as it can illuminate, and he became, as a result, the involuntary founder of a whole school of "debunking" biography. His imitators generally ended by writing biographies which criticized the subjects for leading the lives they did. They captured the worst side of Lytton Strachey and overlooked his best: his accurate perception of character and humanity in his personages. Whatever quarrel we may have with his portrait of Victoria and her consort, we cannot deny the fact that they are living figures—human in the midst of their onerous and often starched responsibilities; they have a vividness which Strachey's imitators seldom achieved. "He maintained," said Edmund Wilson after Strachey's untimely death, "a rare attitude of humility, of astonishment and admiration, before the unpredictable spectacle of life." It is this side of Strachey which is important now. These are the positive elements in his work: his genius for squeezing into a single phrase certain aspects of a person; his capacity for combing great masses of documents to find the substance of that phrase; the skill with which he captures incident and detail in order to light up a scene or to bring a personality into relief; above all the wit and liveliness of his prose by which he lifted biography from plodding narrative into literary expression. It has been said of him that he was the "supreme and perhaps only example of an artist in fiction who naturally expressed his genius in biography," and Harold Nicolson has testified to the other aspect of him, that side which fervently believed in intellectual honesty, with "an almost revivalist dislike of the second-hand, the complacent, or the conventional; a derisive contempt for emotional opinions ... a respect, ultimately, for man's unconquerable mind." Nicolson, I think, does full justice to him; but Strachey's shortcomings have been allowed to tower over his accomplishments, and he has been undone to some extent by his imitators.

And so this third type of biography, striking a middle course between the long, documented life and the portrait, can borrow some of Strachey's theories and methods. In this type the biographer constantly characterizes and comments and analyzes, instead of merely displaying chronologically the contents of a card index or a filing cabinet. "Uninterpreted truth," Strachey said, "is as useless as buried gold; and art is the great interpreter. It alone can unify a vast multitude of facts into a significant whole, clarifying, accentuating, suppressing, and lighting up the dark places of the imagination." Interpretation need not become, however, moral approval or disapproval of the life itself. There enters into the process a quality of sympathy with the subject which is neither forebearance nor adulation; it is quite simply the capacity to be aware at every moment that the subject was human and therefore fallible.

FICTION

I NOW PROPOSE to pause in the midst of these reflections on the nature of biography to discuss a work of fiction. Novelists have often pretended they were writing biographies or autobiographies. This was the method of Daniel Defoe, that mastermingler of truth and fiction; of Dickens in *David Copperfield;* of Sterne in *Tristram Shandy,* the full title of which is *The Life and Opinions of Tristram Shandy, Gentleman.*

On the subject of biography and fiction I have already quoted Hugh Kenner, himself the author of a critical biography of T.S. Eliot entitled *The Invisible Poet,* which I am told Eliot admired. Kenner seeks to perpetuate the offhand views of the New Criticism when he speaks of biography as a minor branch of fiction.

Biography is a minor branch of fiction, of fairly old-fashioned fiction, too. It's hard to think of a biographer's stratagem that hasn't its antecedents in Walter Scott or Dickens. No matter whether you've invented your central character or gleaned his dossier from "sources" you can footnote, what you do next is nothing but tell his story in the way of the Victorian masters. So Joseph Blotner's *Faulkner,* Mark Schorer's *Sinclair Lewis,* Richard Ellmann's *Joyce,* are all for better or worse fictional creations. Each biographer had no choice save to flesh out his man from his idea of his man: from what he was capable of imagining. "Creation of character," it used to be called.

To have a respected critic deliver himself thus will give biographers pause. A second reading of this paragraph reveals however that each sentence is built on a false assumption; and the examples chosen by Kenner happen to be the modern blockbuster biographies which conform to Victorian biography rather than attempt the kinds of biography I have been discussing. Biography cannot be a branch of fiction, for it deals in proveable and palpable fact, or in speculation about these facts after the manner of criticism. In short it is, if anything, a branch of criticism concerned with values and ideas and forms and ways of life not invented by the biographer or the critic. The only resemblance it may have to fiction is that it uses existing form of narration; and these forms can be used in many ways. I find it strange that Kenner, with his study of the moderns, did not mention the more experimental kinds of biography in our century, those which were "composed" rather than shovelled together— Painter's *Proust,* Strachey's *Eminent Victorians* or, indeed, my life of James, which contains many experimental devices; he chose instead three American biographies written in the old-fashioned Victorian chronological manner. As for Kenner's saying that the biographer fleshes out "his man from his ideas of his man" I would suggest that this occurs in those biographies suffering from "transference," but hardly at all in such lives as follow the documented impress made by individuals on their time.

The most competent biographers seek a narrative technique suitable to the subject matter. The mode of telling does not undermine truth nor fact; and the picture of the hero or heroine hews closely to historical memory. Kenner propounds an absurdity; he might as well tell the national portrait galleries that they have on their walls imaginary portraits and that painting is a minor branch of photography.

We are in possession of a ready way to test Kenner's assumptions. There exists a biographical novel written by an eminent novelist, a modern, who also wrote a biography—and in doing the latter clamored for release so she could return to her fiction. This suggests, it seems to me, that a skilled novelist does see a distinct difference between the art of fiction and the art of biography. Virginia Woolf wrote *Orlando* as a piece of fiction based, however, on a life, that of her friend Vita Sackville-West. And then she wrote a life of her friend Roger Fry, the painter and art critic. No critic reading the life of Fry would call it a fiction, even as no one reading *Orlando* would call it a biography. We can test Kenner's observation in this way—and see precisely where the differences are to be found. Since Woolf, who clearly had no illusions about what she was doing, was often as experimental as Joyce in her narrative modes, we can hardly accuse her of imitating Scott or Dickens, who we might add, are often worth emulating.

Let us examine first the book Virginia Woolf called *Orlando: A Biography* in which she reverses Kenner's idea; for she is writing, in a very old tradition, a novel that pretends to be a biography and therefore to be telling the truth.

I

One does not have to read far into *Orlando* to discover that it is a fantasy in the form of a biography. Orlando's longevity is by no means the only unusual thing about him. He starts out as a youth in the Elizabethan age; he arrives in the Victorian, a young woman. The book begins with a modest and slightly farcical acknowledgment, after the manner of ponderous biographies, in which Mrs. Woolf thanks a great many writers for the help they gave her in composing this work. She lists Defoe, Sir Thomas Browne, Sterne, Scott, Macaulay, Emily Brontë and others. There are also friendly acknowledgments to two biographers, Lytton Strachey and Harold Nicolson. In keeping with its nature the volume is endowed with an index. The pretense of scholarship and exactitude is maintained to the end. Yet it is a rather mischievous index, for it supplies data not in the text. Thus early in the book Orlando spies, while dashing through the servants' quarters, a rather fat, shabby man, "whose ruff was a thought dirty, and whose clothes were of hodden brown." He has a tankard of ale beside him and paper in front of him and he seems in the act of rolling some thought up and down. "His eyes, globed and clouded like some green stone of curious texture, were fixed." And Orlando, rushing to offer a bowl of rosewater to the great Queen, has only time to wonder whether this man is a poet who could tell him "everything in the whole world." Only in the index do we discover—though we tend to guess it—that the poet is Shakespeare.

Such then are the conventional trappings which dress out this fantasy-biography. Small wonder that Woolf was promptly asked by the booksellers whether they were to place the book on the fiction or the biography shelf. Mrs. Woolf had a vision of reduced sales because the book was as ambiguous as the sex of its hero-heroine. She wrote in her diary that it was "a high price to pay for the fun of calling it a biography." She did not have to pay the price. The book sold well on both shelves and it is recognized today as containing some of the novelist's most brilliant writing: there are few pages in modern English literature to equal the prose in which the great frost of the Jacobean age is described, or the coming of the cloud that settles over London and brings with it the Victorian century.

For criticism, however, there are more pressing questions than the finding of a proper shelf for *Orlando*. What sort of work is it?—a mere literary lark, a modern allegory, a subtle fable? "The fun of calling it a biography," Virginia Woolf had written. It was "fun" then for the writer. This we can perceive in the exuberant and flashing prose and in the way in which the imagination is allowed to romp from the unexpected to the unexpected. Conventions are mocked, the suffragette question is treated in a vein of satire, and Woolf tries to remind us throughout the book of the androgynous character of human life. Literary pundits are also satirized, and so are critics. Biographers are lectured in long asides on the nature of biography; The book ranges far and wide in its actual story of Orlando. We discover him as a youth slashing at the skull of a Moor in the great house of his ancestors during the reign of Elizabeth I: he is all fire, poetry, passion. He falls in love during the reign of James with a Muscovite princess who is visiting England. The Thames freezes over and great spectacles and ceremonies are held on the ice. The princess proves fickle. Orlando tries to mend his broken heart and find solace in literature. Throughout the book he is attempting to write a long poem called *The Oak Tree*. In due course he is named ambassador to Turkey, and this gives Virginia Woolf an opportunity to mock the life of high diplomacy. Orlando somewhere along the way marries a gypsy, Rosina Pepita; and then, after falling into a trance during a period of riot and massacre, awakens to discover that there has been a great alteration. He had gone to sleep an ambassador. He awakens an ambassadress; but since the embassy is no more, as a result of the riots, the female Orlando goes off to live among gypsies. Homeward bound, she begins to discover how pleasant it is to receive gallant and even amorous attention from men, and in particular the ship's captain. When she lands, England has reached the eighteenth century. There is a great lawsuit to determine her rights to the male Orlando's extensive properties. She pours tea for Addison, for Dr. Johnson, for Mr. Pope at different times during the century, but decides they do not really like women. And so she lives into the century of Victoria, accepts domesticity, falls in love, marries, has a son, and eventually she is riding in trains and driving a car. Having spanned centuries, Virginia Woolf in the end pinpoints the moment: it is midnight, 11 October 1928—the clocks chime the hour and the book ends.

II

Some critics treated this novel as extravaganza; others studied it as a serious piece of fiction to be equated with Woolf's other novels. One critic failed entirely to see the humor of the work saying "we miss the personal touch, the note of passion and pity which raised the novels to tragic heights." But we know, now that we have Virginia Woolf's diary, how she felt. There was no tragic intention, no desire to write a *Mrs. Dalloway* or *To the Lighthouse*. She was having fun—creating a joke. The word "splash" occurs again and again. She writes at one point that Orlando is "too thin—a joke—splashed over the canvas."

And again: "half laughing, half serious: with great splashes of exaggeration."

Or again: "I have scrambled and splashed." Orlando was thus *splashwork*: it was Virginia Woolf liberating herself, letting herself go, as she was doing in her affair with Vita. At another moment she saw Orlando as "too long for a joke, and too frivolous for a serious book." "The canvas shows through in a thousand places." It was an escapade, a satire in spirit, "structure wild." "It is all a joke; and yet gay and quick reading I think: a writer's holiday." But finally "Orlando taught me how to write a direct sentence; taught me continuity and narrative, and how to keep the realities at bay." It was an experiment in fictional biography—but based on a real life and it incorporated all the significant moments, the great crises in Vita Sackville-West's life.

This means that Orlando can be read as a *livre à clé*. The key is placed by Woolf in the reader's hand. The original edition contained four photographs of Vita Sackville-West and it was abundantly clear, even from a superficial examination of the work, that in describing Orlando's country house with its three hundred and sixty-five rooms, the author had described closely, if in an exaggerated manner, the essential aspects of Knole, the country house of Sir Thomas Sackville and his descendants. The book is in part a pastiche of Sackville family history and a scarcely concealed biographical sketch, genealogy and all, of Vita Sackville-West (to whom it is dedicated). Her grandmother was Pepita, the gypsy, and her grandparents were involved in an elaborate suit over the legitimacy of the children of Lionel Sackville-West and Pepita. Vita Sackville-West was the author of a poem, *The Land,* which is Orlando's poem *The Oak Tree.* And if we read carefully we can find that Woolf included

Vita's transvestite affair with Violet Trefusis which Nigel
Nicolson disclosed in *Portrait of a Marriage* (1973).

This then is the more manifest material in the book.
It is equally clear that within it Virginia Woolf was
sketching, in a poetic fashion, the changing temper of
English literature and the changing aspects of the English
social scene between Elizabethan days and modern times,
and the role of the man of letters from the time of
Shakespeare to the time of Lytton Strachey. At every
turn we discover her lively imagination pulling together
many of the threads that fashioned the contemporary
English mind.

If we go outside the book to seek its history, we come
upon still more curious matters, a veritable network of
biographers. The idea for the work was given to Virginia Woolf by Lytton Strachey. One day at lunch he
told her that he felt she was not yet master of her fictional method—this was apropos of *Mrs. Dalloway.* He
suggested (and she put it into her diary): "You should
take something wilder and more fantastic, a framework
that admits of anything, like *Tristram Shandy."* This fictional biography thus was originally proposed by a
preeminent figure in modern biography. The acknowledgment, as we have seen, carries not only Strachey's
name, but also that of another biographer, Harold
Nicolson, who was to write a little volume on biography
published by Leonard and Virginia Woolf at the Hogarth
Press. The plot thickens considerably when we note that
Nicolson's wife is none other than Vita Sackville-West.
And if we remind ourselves that Virginia Woolf's father,
Sir Leslie Stephen, was the editor of the *Dictionary of
National Biography,* we have a vision of Orlando, grand-
fathered and uncled by a group of biographers.

Is it any wonder then that embedded in this would-be biography is a full-fledged theory of biography, and that the book seems to be saying a great deal about this art or science or craft—saying it to the shade of Sir Leslie, to Strachey, to Nicolson and using Vita's family history as its subject? *Orlando* is in reality neither a literary joke nor entirely a novel: it belongs to another *genre*. It is a fable—a fable for biographers, embodying those views of biography which had often been exchanged among the Bloomsbury group, but to which are now added a series of commentaries and illustrations by Woolf. The work speaks for a looser, freer kind of biography. In a letter to Sackville-West, Woolf spoke of trying to "revolutionize biography in a night."

She hardly started a revolution, but her book has been inviting biographers to read and study it for many years. *Orlando*'s central and gentlest mockery is of time and of history: its insistent theme is that human time does not accord with clock time, and that our mechanical way of measuring the hours makes no allowance for the richness of life embodied in a given moment, which can hold within it the experience of decades. Clocks may chime in Edwardian or Georgian England or in the England of Elizabeth II, but they are chiming in an England that was also the England of Elizabeth I. Are there not great houses like Knole still standing with their backward reach to the other time, with rooms in which the present holds the past in a tight embrace? Lady Nicolson's own account of Knole mentions chairs, stools, sofas, love-seats with their original coverings untouched, "but merely softened into greater loveliness by time." She goes on: "They stand beneath the portraits of the men and women who sat in them; the great four-poster beds still stand in the rooms of the men and women who slept in them, drawing the curtains closely round them at night to keep out the cold. The very hairbrushes are still on the dressing tables"; and the very people of today, like Vita Sackville-West, is not their backward reach to the ancestry that lived in such a house as close and as real?

Does this not mean that the biography of any individual must be recreated out of a total past and not merely out of the mechanical calendar-present of their lives? It is by this route that we come to an even deeper level in *Orlando:* for while Virginia Woolf attached her story to fragments from the life of her friend Lady Nicolson, what she is telling us also in this book is the story of her own life. She appears to be saying that when she was young and at liberty in Leslie Stephen's great library, her imaginative life was identified with the Elizabethans; she too could experience the vigorous sensual life of the age, glimpsing the great figures and winning favor at the court of Elizabeth; all her readings of the old writers had so much reality for her that they came to be a part of her own life. Perhaps *she* had slashed at the head of a Moor and had adventures on the frozen Thames and loved a beautiful princess from Muscovy. Then, growing older, she was disturbed as a young woman by the tyranny of sex when she found herself at large in a man's world. At the same time she was an individual who had absorbed her nation's literature and traditions and this made her one with her land. She was England and all that it had been. In this sense may not an artist speak for a nation's androgyny as well as its cultural and historical heritage? May not the artist possess instead of femininity or masculinity the very stuff and fiber of a people, indeed both the masculine and the feminine qualities of England's greatness? A biographer attempting to deal strictly with the facts of Virginia Woolf's life

[193

would miss this rich fabric woven into the deepest parts of her consciousness, past and present, and would reduce her to a line drawing or a caricature rather than capture the many selves of which she was the composite.

What are some of the asides in *Orlando* on the subject of biography? I have already quoted a few: "that riot and confusion of the passions and emotions which every good biographer detests"—this is but one of Woolf's many jibes at conventional biographers. At another moment she suggests that a biographer must keep pace with the development of the personality he is recreating; she wonders also whether this can really be accomplished; it involves keeping pace not only with an individual but with those many selves which we are within our consti-tuted self. She speaks of the "first duty of a biographer" and mockingly describes it as "to plod without looking to right or left, in the indelible footprints of truth; unen-ticed by flowers; regardless of shade, on and on method-ically"—and here she echoes Strachey—"till we fall plump into the grave and write finis on the tombstone above our heads." (Strachey's passage, in the preface to *Emi-nent Victorians,* has been quoted many times and yet I cannot resist repeating it at this point: "With us," wrote Strachey of Victorian biography, "the most delicate and humane of all the branches of the art of writing has been relegated to the journeymen of letters; we do not reflect that it is perhaps as difficult to write a good life as to live one." And he continued: "Those two fat volumes, with which it is our custom to commemorate the dead— who does not know them, with their ill-digested masses of material, their slipshod style, their tone of tedious panegyric, their lamentable lack of selection, of detach-ment, of design. They are as familiar as the cortege of the undertaker, and wear the same air of slow, funereal barbarism.")

Virginia Woolf in *Orlando* seems to have Strachey constantly in mind. The biographer, she says, is a votary of Truth, Candor and Honesty, "the austere Gods who keep watch and ward by the inkpot of biography," and at the moment of Orlando's change of sex these three engage in a duel with Purity, Modesty and Chastity. Their insistent trumpetings that the truth be told finally prevail. Later we discover that biographers and historians in Woolf's view are not capable of writing truthful accounts of London society, "for only those who have little need of the truth and no respect for it—the poets and the novelists—can be trusted to do it, for this is one of the cases where the truth does not exist." The undercurrent of Woolf's argument is that we live in a solipsistic universe and that the only truth we know is that which lies within the envelope of personal consciousness. To the attempt to describe this evanescent universe she is wholly dedicated. There are passages in *Orlando* on the sexlessness of biographers and historians, on the helplessness of the biographer faced with thought and emotion in the given subject, on the biographical reliance on "perhaps" and "it appears"—and when we have made our way through the book and added up these numerous asides we must recognize that at the heart of Virginia Woolf's argument is the question of time. Here she is at one with all her contemporaries—those who have written novels since Bergson—Proust and Joyce, Dorothy Richardson and William Faulkner. What they have tried to do in fiction, that is, record man's sense of time, psychological and human, as distinct from clock time, she feels to be an attempt that belongs also to the field of biography. She writes in *Orlando:*

An hour, once it lodges in the queer element of the human spirit, may be stretched to fifty or a hundred times its clock length; on the other hand, an hour may be accurately represented on the timepiece of the mind by one second. This extraordinary discrepancy between time on the clock and time in the mind is less known than it should be and deserves fuller investigation. But the biographer, whose interests are, as we have said, highly restricted, must confine himself to one simple statement: when a man has reached the age of thirty, as Orlando now had, time when he is thinking becomes inordinately long; time when he is doing becomes inordinately short. Thus Orlando gave his orders and did the business of his vast estates in a flash; but directly he was alone on the mound under the oak tree, the seconds began to round and fill until it seemed as if they would never fall.

So far as I am aware, few biographers have listened to the fable Virginia Woolf created for them—a work whimsical and mocking and idiosyncratic, and yet filled with many wonderful flashes of truth—because *Orlando* belongs to the shelf of fiction! It is clear that the biographer cannot do all that Woolf would like done. Biography, unlike fiction, cannot get into the stream of consciousness of its subject; indeed even fiction can at best arrive only at a simulation of the stream of thought or perceptual experience. But most novelists would have no argument with Virginia Woolf over the question of time. A biography attached to the calendar or the clock risks becoming monotonous. Chronological biography tends to fragment and flatten a life. However, on occasion the chronological method is called for by the material. Rupert Hart-Davis's biography of Hugh Walpole, dealing with the likeable storyteller whose life was a continual success story, gave us the recurrent pattern, year by year, of this success. Walpole did indeed live life as if it were a constant engagement book. On the other hand, there are biographies in which the year-in-year-out formula isolates episodes and ideas, and scatters them through time when they should be brought together. Let me once more use an example from my life of Henry James, in the volume titled *The Conquest of London.*

In scanning Henry James's life during the years that followed his first adult journey to Europe, I came upon the following sentence in a letter to Grace Norton, his Cambridge friend. "I spent lately," wrote the future novelist, "a couple of days with Mr. Emerson at Concord—pleasantly but with slender profit." That is all. Were I writing the chronicle type of biography I would quote this at the proper calendar date, September 1870. This would convey to the reader the simple historical fact: the future novelist spent a couple of days—slenderly profitable—with Ralph Waldo Emerson in his Concordian setting. Two years later in my chronicle I would mention that Henry James met Mr. Emerson in Paris. They visited the Louvre together. A few months later I would report that they met in Rome. They spent a morning together looking at the sculptures in the Vatican. When I reach the year 1883, when Henry James has become famous, I would chronicle the fact that he journeys once again to Concord, this time to attend Mr. Emerson's funeral. And in my chronicle I would in due course mention James's reviews of the Carlyle-Emerson correspondence in 1883 and describe an article on Emerson which James published in December of 1887.

Why did James write this article in the year 1887? It was not because at this moment he felt prompted to recapture the image of his departed friend. There was a fortuitous circumstance. The essay was occasioned by the publication of the Cabot memoir of Emerson. Although

James was writing it in 1887, his actual relationship with his subject belongs, as we have seen, to an earlier period. Yet the chronicle biography would deal with the essay under 1887, validly enough, although the date is an accidental one. On the other hand, when James visited Emerson in Concord seventeen years before, he was in relation with a man he had known from early childhood, whose work he had read and admired. He had heard him lecture; he was familiar with his life at Concord; he had met or known through Henry James Senior some of the men and women who surrounded Emerson. Emerson thus was not merely an august figure in the life of Henry James, an elder man of letters. He was woven into the fabric of James's consciousness and into James's life, not at the precise chronological moments that I happen to know about because certain records have been preserved; there were many other moments, moments perhaps of greater importance, for which we do not have the record. He is represented in James's life not only as a figure encountered now and again during four decades, but as a veritable symbol, a revered and noble presence, a voice rich with the many tones of New England. When they went to look at the pictures in the Louvre, there was, in the consciousness of James an increasingly composite figure, which was the Emerson of all the years he had known him—the Emerson in his prime, the Emerson in his old age. And when the final respects were paid to him at the grave, a summarized Emerson existed in his mind whom he could evoke, piecing together the Emerson of his memories: the benevolent, sparse figure of the Fourteenth Street hearthside, the man who read his Boston Hymn at the moment of the emancipation of the slaves, the rural figure in his homely setting—indeed the man in all the decades as Henry James had known him. Now, what was important for James: these pleasant encounters, of which there may have been many more than we know, or the man and what he stood for, and his work, to which James returned at various times with unmistakable pleasure, and the qualities, as well as the defects, he discerned in the eminent personality?

The essay of 1887 gives us the picture. I shall string together a few random sentences.

Emerson's personal history is condensed into a single word Concord, and all the condensation in the world will not make it look rich. ... Passions, alternations, affairs, adventures had absolutely no part in it. It stretched itself out in enviable quiet—a quiet in which we hear the jotting of the pencil in the notebook. ... The plain, God-fearing, practical society which surrounded him was not fertile in variations. On three occasions later—three journeys to Europe—he was introduced to a more complicated world; but his spirit, his moral taste, as it were, abode always within the undecorated walls of his youth. There he could dwell with that ripe unconsciousness of evil which is one of the most beautiful signs by which we know him.

There are many more such sentences in the essay, and if we read them, and read between the lines, they tell us much of Henry James's observation of Emerson and his feelings for him and his surroundings. And they tell us much about Henry James, for we see the values and the judgments James invoked in assessing Emerson's role in American life and letters. How much of James's own awareness is implied in that phrase about Emerson's "ripe unconsciousness of evil". We are provided with ample material to enable us to evaluate the friendship, to form a picture in our mind, and even to create a biographical scene. In my mind all this material melted together into a portrait of the two, the young man and the old, the one at the beginning of his career, the other near the end, in Concord, at the Louvre, at the Vatican. I place my scene in Concord in 1870—for this is where Emerson belonged and where both can best be placed in their American setting. In that scene I show James, young, earnest, brimming over with his recent European journey; Emerson, old, but not yet suffering from the amnesia of his later years, moving in his contrasted world, the fields and orchards of Concord. In creating this scene I violate no fact. I put no thoughts into James's head or into Emerson's. I adhere to the one point of view in my possession, James's, and try to set down his vision and perception—which he recorded— of the man of Concord. But from Concord I leap into the future, to Europe and back again, and to the past, and back again, and to the funeral, and to Concord again as Henry James viewed it when he himself was old, thirty-five years later, and long after it had taken its cherished place in American literary history. Henry James wrote in 1907 that "not a russet leaf fell for me, while I was there, but fell with an Emersonian drop."

I do this in violation of all chronology, dealing with my subject's relation to Emerson at the most meaningful moment that I can find—the moment when Henry James is taking the measure of America and deciding whether he will remain in that country or yield to his cosmopolitanism. Instead of chronicling little episodes and encounters piecemeal, as mere anecdotes, I recreate two personalities in their relationship to one another and in particular the significance of the older man to the younger. By weaving backward and forward in time and even dipping into the future, which to us, as readers, is after

all entirely of the past, I reckon with time as it really
exists, as something fluid and irregular and with memory, as something alive and flickering and evanescent. I
refuse to be fettered by the clock and the calendar. I
neither depart from my documents nor do I disparage
them. Ultimately I, as the biographer, must paint the
portrait and I can paint it only from the angle of vision
I have, and from my time and its relation to the time
that I seek to recover. If I paint carefully, and do my
utmost not to falsify the colors, there is no reason why I
should not in the end be able to hang before my reader
a reasonable likeness, which is all that a biographer can
hope to achieve—instead of offering him a card index,
a cluttered worktable, or a figure of papier-mâché.

III

The scenic method in literary biography recommends
itself to us for a number of reasons, and largely because,
in addition to being a dramatic method, it enables us to
convey more easily the passage of time. As we construct
scene after scene, each composed of those moments which
we can document, we gain the sense of being in a con-
tinuum instead of in separated moments. It is a little like
the sense we have if we go to the same place every summer, of having been in that place continuously for a long
time. What happens is that the intervening winter months
fade away and the successive summers are melded
together. The biographical edifice stands much more
firmly when it is built in this fashion; the biographer
does not indulge in the false pretense of reconstructing
every minute, but instead creates a time-atmosphere akin
to that created by the novelist. The more loosely written
work offers bits and scraps of fact and quotations from

documents without any genuine integration. The biographer happens to know that Byron saw his mistress on one day, went hunting on the next, mourned at the burial of his favorite hound, and then wrote a letter sympathizing with a friend who had a death in his family. A chronological recital of these facts reads like a newspaper; we jump from one item to another, and the items seem unrelated. But if the story about the mistress is assembled in one place; if at the right moment we glimpse the poet as huntsman or as animal lover, and if we see him in his relationships with his friends, we give to his life a dramatic quality rather than offering a recital of little disconnected facts.

In a sense what I am proposing is that the biographer borrow some of the techniques of fiction without lapsing into fiction. A tedious recital of biographical data may still have much life in it when the subject offers a rich mind and an abundance of rich quotation; but it also makes us all the more aware of how much vividness can be lost in the process. What happens often is that the scholar who has carried out the research is not necessarily a writer, and lacks the style and the touch that can do justice to his subject. Devotion to the art of expression is needed, and it quite often does not match the devotion to the search for biographical truth. The best one can hope for in such cases is a sober massing of the data, and at least a genuine organization of it. The book then becomes a source book for another and more expert writer who will ultimately be master of this material rather than mastered by it.

On the subject of biography and the novel André Maurois had many interesting things to say in his Clark Lectures. Having written fiction and fictionalized biography before he became a serious biographer, he appreciated the need for striking a balance between the novelist's imaginative freedom and the biographer's factual boundaries. But he saw also what few biographers see, that there is such a thing as finding the ideal form for this factual material. Maurois observes that in *War and Peace,* Tolstoy is able to give Napoleon a vividness he cannot have in the pages of history. Writing as a novelist, not as an historian, Tolstoy can describe Napoleon stretching out his small, chubby hand or casting a glance at the tsar, impart to him moments of emotion and relationships with various personages utterly impossible to the historian. Particular vividness is obtained, however, because at certain moments we see Napoleon, in this novel, through the eyes of characters such as Prince Andrey; and if we have achieved empathy with the Prince, it is almost as if *we* were looking at Napoleon.

This is a highly suggestive thought. Why should not biographers weigh with great care experiments in "point of view"? Why should they not find, if possible, various angles of vision, so that their subject, instead of being flattened out, attains a three-dimensional quality. Diaries sometimes make this possible; and sometimes letters or memoirs. Biography, in its fear of fiction, has not studied sufficiently, it seems to me, the possible technical borrowings it can make from that characteristic literary form. There remains much room for trial and experiment in biographical narration.

FACT

Discussing the art of fiction, Henry James pointed out long ago that the story and the novel, the idea and the form, are like a needle and thread, and he added, "I never heard of a guild of tailors who recommended the use of thread without the needle, or the needle without the thread." In biography, selection and design are the needle and thread; and those scholars who see their biography as materials to be set down in rigid chronologies end up not with a garment on their hands but with the bolts of cloth and boxes of buttons. There has been no sewing. And then there are biographers who, when they sew, sew on too many buttons, and employ too many stitches. We have, in other words, biographies which are content without form, whereas in the work of art, content and form are one and inseparable. This is the very heart of our problem.

I

As there are many kinds of tailors so are there many kinds of biographers, and the dilemma of their art is that to write a biography they must establish a proper relationship between that which is research and scholarship, and that which is narrative. What is required on the one hand is a careful subordination of research, which is the kitchen work of biography, to art. How achieve the happy medium? How be at once nimble and creative, large in imagination, while at the same time plodding in detail? How be inventive—and yet not invent? We are fortunate in having an illuminating example. Virginia Woolf was a gifted and sentient novelist; the novel was her medium; she envisaged it as a kind of prose poem. And yet this woman, so filled with poetry, could not keep her hands off the prose of the biography. The writing of lives haunted her; she set down brilliant essays on the subject and she discussed it with Lytton Strachey. In her diary she tells herself:

> It is a good idea to write biographies; to make them use my powers of representing reality, and accuracy; and to use my novels simply to express the general, the poetic.

The moment came when she decided to turn from her novels to write a life; not a fictional life, one like *Orlando*, but the story of a man who had lived in her own time, a man older than herself and one whom she had known. He was an artist and a considerable force in the art world of two continents. Roger Fry died in 1934 and Virginia Woolf went to his funeral. Returning she noted in her diary that the service had consisted simply of music and added that there had been "something ripe and musical about him—and then the fun and the fact that he had lived with such variety and generosity and curiosity." When she wrote this she little dreamed how involved her own life would become with his, and that there would be, as she later observed, a posthumous friendship more intimate than any she had had with him in life. In the year after his death she begins to read his letters and his miscellaneous journalism. Three years later she has worked her way through these materials: she feels that she is ready to start her book. "Much of it is donkey work," she notes, "sober drudgery." We may well imagine this. For a novelist to be pinioned to documents must be a hardship indeed, a harnessing of fancy to fact. A month after starting: "I am a little appalled at the prospect of the grind this book will be." Entries in her diaries tell a vivid story: the novelist trapped in the machinery of biography:

> May 5, 1938—What about all the letters? How can one cut loose from facts, when there they are, contradicting my theories.
>
> July 7, 1938—Oh the appalling grind of getting back to Roger! ... How can I concentrate upon minute facts in letters? It's all too minute and tied down—documented. Is it to be done on this scale? Is he interesting to other people in that light? I think I will go on doggedly till I meet him myself—1909—and then attempt something more fictitious. But must plod on through all these letters till then.

The artist is enmeshed in documents; tied down, she says, wanting to cut loose. And what is more, she is writing the life of a critic and a painter, and this is even more difficult than writing the life of a writer. For paintings are translated into words with difficulty; and the stuff of criticism involves intellectual concepts and formulations which must be dealt with, but which can also be stumbling blocks in trying to keep before the reader moments of feeling as well as intellect.

> Aug. 17, 1938—No, I won't go on doing Roger—abstracting with blood and sweat from the old Articles—right up to lunch. I will steal 25 minutes. In fact I've been getting absorbed in *Roger*. Didn't I say I wouldn't? Didn't L[eonard]

say there's no hurry? Except that I'm 56 ... A tearing wind last night. Every sort of scenic effect—a prodigious toppling and clearing and massing, after the sunset that was so amazing L. made me come and look out of the bathroom window—a flurry of red clouds; hard; a water colour mass of purple and black, soft as a water ice; then hard slices of intense green stone; blue stone and ripple of crimson light. No: that won't convey it: and then there were the trees in the garden; and the reflected light ...

The pen can cut loose and describe wind and color and clouds, and try to capture what the eye has seen and what has been felt: but how capture the color of letters, documents, old articles, an "abstraction with blood and sweat"?

The time comes, however, when the novelist goes to work on the biographical material. The discipline of craft is brought to bear on her task:

Suppose I make a break after H's death. A separate paragraph quoting what R. himself said. Then a break. Then begin definitely with the first meeting. That is the first impression: a man of the world, not professor or Bohemian. Then give facts in his letters to his mother. Then back to the second meeting. Pictures: talk about art: I look out of window. His persuasiveness—a certain density— wished to persuade you to like what he liked. Eagerness, absorption, stir—a kind of vibration like a hawkmoth round him. Or shall I make a scene here—at Ott[oline's]? Then Constantinople. Driving out; getting things in: his deftness in combining. Then quote the letters to R.

This is method—a search for ways of marrying form and content, but also the direct use of personal memory as well.

Oct. 6, 1938—Head screwed up over Roger.

Jan. 8th, 1939—Now that I have brought my brain to the state of an old washerwoman's flannel over *Roger*—Lord the Josette chapter—and it's all too detailed, too tied down—I must expand . . . in fiction. Though I've ground out most wish to write even fiction.

March 11th, 1939—Yesterday . . . I set the last word to the first sketch of *Roger*. And now I have to begin—well not even to begin, but to revise and revise. A terrible grind to come: and innumerable doubts, of myself as biographer; of the possibility of doing it all: all the same I've carried through to the end; and may allow myself one moment's mild gratification. There are the facts more or less extracted. And I've no time to go into all the innumerable horrors. There may be a flick of life in it—or is it all dust and ashes?

April 15th, 1939—I've done rather well at *Roger* considering: I don't think I shall take two weeks over each chapter. And it's rather amusing—dealing drastically with this year's drudgery. I think I see how it shapes: and my compiling method was a good one. Perhaps it's too like a novel?

April 26th, 1939—What a grind it is; and I suppose of little interest except to six or seven people. And I shall be abused.

June 29th, 1939—The grind of doing *Roger*. . .

She persists. Work done is work done, grind or no grind.

This gifted woman was caught between her leaping imagination and mundane fact. "How glad I am to escape to my free page," she notes at last, when her book is done. And what sort of biography emerged from this grind? It is lucid; precise; there is no irrelevancy; we may sense in some moments that she resists this kind of writing. In the first half of the book in the years before she knew Roger Fry, she writes the kind of biography which may be studied for its summarizing quality, its constant reaching for essence. The narrative is orderly and meticulous, as if the attic is being emptied of its clutter. Everything is placed in its place. To the outsider, the person not interested in Roger Fry, and in the post-impressionists, the story here may be a little dull; but it comes to life in those episodes in which we see Fry in action. When he travels with J.P. Morgan to Italy as consultant and watches the millionaire's quest for art, we have a dramatic episode. Here Virginia Woolf lets Fry be the narrator, and she uses the diary or journal form effectively. But whatever the work's shortcomings, one is struck by the writer's grasp of her materials; the "grind" is concealed behind organization and order.

Often in later life Roger Fry was to deplore the extraordinary indifference of the English to the visual arts, and their determination to harness all art to moral problems. Among the undergraduates of his day, even the most thoughtful, the most speculative, this indifference seems to have been almost universal. His own interest in abstract argument was so keen that the deficiency scarcely made itself felt then. But as his letters show, even while they argued his eye was always active. He noticed the changing lights on the willows, the purple of the thunderstorm on the grey stone of the colleges, the sunset lights on the flat fields. Many half sheets are filled with careful architectural drawings.

This is excellent biographical narrative; the biographer communicates a series of facts about her subject with the economy of art. We are made aware of that mixture of abstract intellectualism that was part of being a Cambridge undergraduate, and the eye of the artist that looked upon the world even while partaking of abstract discussion. It is also the biographer having the courage not to be compulsive: we can imagine an academic biographer, who knows only his documents, producing a letter and a date to give us the intellectual discussion; and another letter and a date to show us the poetry in Roger Fry; and perhaps another to act as illustration and show his architectural drawings.

We may imagine how many letters Woolf read in order to write the following passage, in which she lays aside her data and asks herself the significant question: what did France mean to Roger Fry?

> Italy, as the skipping summary of the letters is enough to show, was a lovely land of brilliant light and clear outlines; it was a place where one worked hard all day seeing Old Masters; where one settled down at night in some little pub to sample strange dishes and to argue with other English travellers about art. But it was not a place with a living art and a living civilization that one could share with the Italians themselves. France was to be that country. He was to spend his happiest days there, he was to find his greatest inspiration as a critic there. But he seems in 1892 to have had no premonition what France was to mean to him, and for perhaps the last time in his life he exclaimed on leaving Paris, "It'll be ripping to see London and its inhabitants again."

The biographer has the courage to ask a question and seek its answer at a logical place in her narrative— a place in the development of her hero, and in a chapter called *London: Italy: Paris*. In the paragraph I have quoted she is in the year 1892, but she jumps into the future, lifts the curtain a little, because she is not going to pretend that Roger Fry is at a given age in any part of the book. He is Roger Fry, the subject of her biography; and when we glimpse him as a boy, we know the man he became; and when he is still an impatient young man in Paris, she knows, and we know, that Paris will come to be that center from which all his work on the post-impressionists will stem. Time, for Virginia Woolf, is fluid in this biography; that is why there is the time-pulse in her sentences and paragraphs.

It takes many letters and much search among journals and private papers and published writings—and above all the splendid gift of abstraction—to tell us in a "skipping summary" what Italy and France meant to Roger Fry. This is the art of the précis as Woolf practiced it; and to her it was a "grind." There comes a moment in the book when the novelist is free—for a little while. The biography begins to quiver with new life, it takes on those qualities which animate Boswell's story when we have the feeling of being in direct communion with the subject; it is reminiscence, to be sure, and not all biographers are as fortunate in having such direct observation.

To a stranger meeting him then for the first time [thus Woolf begins her chapter on the postimpressionists, and she is writing of 1910] he looked much older than his age. He was only forty-four, but he gave the impression of a man with a great weight of experience behind him. He looked worn and seasoned, ascetic yet tough. And there was his reputation, of course, to confuse a first impression—his reputation as a lecturer and as an art critic. He did not live up to his reputation, if one expected a man who lectured upon the Old Masters at Leighton House to be pale, academic, aesthetic looking. On the contrary, he

was brown and animated. Nor was he altogether a man of
the world, or a painter—there was nothing Bohemian about
him. It was difficult at first sight to find his pigeonhole.

She goes on to seek it: Fry's talk, his voice; it is easy to
make him laugh; yet he is grave. There are his glasses
and his bushy brows.

.... he had very luminous eyes with a curious power of
observation in them as if, while he talked, he looked, and
considered what he saw. Half-consciously he would stretch
out a hand and begin to alter the flowers in a vase, or pick
up a bit of china, turn it round and put it down again.
That look, that momentary detachment, was so instinctive
that it made no break in what he was saying, yet it gave a
sense of something held in reserve—things played over the
surface and were referred to some hidden center. There
was something stable under his mobility.

We see him here; and he is also characterized; it has
required but one or two touches—the hand reaching out
to rearrange the flowers, the eyes mingling with the talk;
and then Virginia Woolf must give us the sense of the
talk—

He was just off—was it to Paris or to Poland? He had to
catch a train. He seemed used to catching trains whether
to Poland or to Paris. It was only for a week or so, and
then he would be back. Out came a little engagement book.
The pages were turned rapidly. He murmured in his deep
voice through a long list of engagements, and at last chose
a day and noted it . . .

And so on. This is the novelist in the role of biographer
at a point where the two meet. Both are storytellers. But
she is not writing fiction.

II

What lesson can we disengage from Virginia Woolf's experience? Novelists, as we are aware, try to persuade their readers that they are writing about a real world and that their people are real—although "any resemblance to persons living or dead is coincidental." We read fiction knowing it to be make-believe, but with a feeling that it isn't—depending on the extent to which the writer has succeeded in making us feel that it isn't. Biographers, however, do not have to indulge in this pretence. The biographer writes about real people; and about things which happened in a world that really was. Truth may be stranger than fiction; and because it is the truth, certain biographers seem to think that it can be offered to the world in a kind of documentary dullness, and with the sobriety of a legal brief. And critics seem to think that because it is the truth, there is no question of art involved.

There seems to me to be no reason why we should not ask that a biography be told with all the art we demand of the novelist, rather than in a dreary, dull recital in which the pages bulge with facts—and those facts which are left over are crowded into the footnotes. To say this, however, is still to speak of biography as a form of artisanry. We must remember one thing: that like the novel or the painting, biography is truth seen (as Zola put it for fiction) through a given temperament. Biography is most itself then when it is a life offered us through a personal vision. The portrait painter does not see a skeleton wrapped in flesh which houses a series of organs and blood vessels. The painter looks on a constructed, palpable being, an individual visible to all, possessed of mannerisms, gestures, facial expressions, tics, clothes. An artist is aware of the anatomy behind the garments, but this is not what is painted in a portrait. The figure set on canvas is the same figure that has been confronting the world.

So the biographer must see the subject not as if it were the contents of a filing cabinet but as part of what these contents represent: a figure good or evil, and if a diminished figure, we must have it in its depravity as we have other figures in their nobility. And even as novelists and painters learn their art by a long process of trial and error, so biographers will have to learn to take their work seriously and stop shovelling materials into dustbins. Today they serve too little apprenticeship. Many are and remain amateurs, biographers of occasion, chroniclers by accident; they think too little about art and talk too much about objective fact as if facts were as hard as bricks or stones. In biography they have never been as hard as that: they are always as soft as flesh, and as yielding.

PART TWO

The Personal Workshop

I AM appending to my discussion of the New Biography three papers of a more personal nature. These tell in a broad and general way the story of my "serialized" life of Henry James which appeared in five volumes between 1953 and 1972; some of the journeys I undertook while writing this work; and the way I assembled one of my chapters out of a few fragments—a little like trying to reconstruct a head or arms for a dismembered statue. Every biographer has such stories and it has seemed to me useful to round out the present volume in this way as representing phases of one biographer's work. Those who have read Richard Altick's *The Scholar Adventurers* or his *Art of Literary Research* or James Clifford's *From Puzzles to Portraits* will realize that I am adding here to the literature of "quest" which I presume to have a certain interest for those who like to hear workshop stories—craftsmen's talk about craft.

Writing the Quintet

ON JANUARY 12, 1971 a winter's day much like any other in New York, I rose at six, prepared my breakfast, glanced at the front page of the *Times,* and sat down at my typewriter. For fifteen of the twenty years I had worked on my five-volume life of Henry James—I emulate Lawrence Durrell and call it my "James Quintet"— I had sat in this room or the adjoining one and looked out over rooftops: a very Londonish view for Manhattan. In recent years the high-rises at the end of the street had chiseled away great chunks of my sky and diminished the flushed dawns or the gray filtered smoggy mornings of other years.

The buildings, it occurred to me, had taken much less time to blot out the sky than I had taken to write my book. I was near the end—the final pages of the final volume. When I sat down that morning, I wasn't sure how far I'd get; one is never sure in advance. The typewriter has a way (for me at least), of going on an unscheduled romp; at such moments one's fingertips seem to be not one's own. (I am, by the way, a two-finger typist.) Three days earlier, addressing a group of English teachers at City University, I had boasted my book would be finished by Thursday (the 14th). This was Tuesday.

I'd been writing, as they say, at a feverish pace. From

the previous October I had felt that all my mental lines were connected; the threads by which my chapters were bound to all the volumes I had written before, all the way back to 1950, were gathered in my hands. Memory and association seemed to be turning up everything I needed. No one who has not written this kind of long-scale work can understand its complexity: it is as if you possess a mental switchboard. Everything went very straight the further I went.

I always write a chapter without knowing what the next one will be.

I try to write without consulting my material; this avoids interruption and prevents me from overloading my text with quotations. In this way, I establish a comfortable distance from the mass and pressure of data. It helps the narrative flow; it is a guard against irrelevancies. I have always argued that compendia biographies are not in reality "written." They are simply a "showing" of bits of letters and "facts" as in a glass case. The way to write a biography, I hold, is to tell the story as much as possible in a direct way, and in the biographer's words.

A biographer is primarily a storyteller. In this I differ from my illustrious predecessor in the art, James Boswell, who pretended he wasn't telling a story at all, but only letting Dr. Johnson speak for himself. Artless Boswell! When the Yale documents are completely known, I am certain they will reveal what a consummate arranger Boswell was: how he stage-managed his hero. Boswell also said he was opposed to "melting down" his materials. I wonder what he would do if he were writing the biography of another member of the Johnson clan, in that brand new library in Texas; how would he cope with the millions of pages, the videotapes and photographs, the endless memorabilia? He would need a thousand volumes. The modern biographer, as I often say, must melt down his materials or be smothered by them.

James lived nearly seventy-three years, and had a large career; he wrote for fifty years. He had known all literary Europe. In consequence, I had to deal with a celebrated cast—Flaubert, Zola, Turgenev, George Eliot, George Meredith, Trollope, the major and minor Victorians, down through the Edwardians to the nascent Bloomsbury group. He had left New York—his birthplace—when it was a provincial city, and lived a full life in the wide world. He loomed very large in our literature, which is but two hundred years old, compared with England's thousand years. In the scale of our two centuries, and in the history of the novel, James preempted a distinctive and a distinguished place: he was craftsman, critic, creator. I said as much when I started my work. He was massive; he would need a large canvas.

I can't now recall the three hours of work I did on Jan. 12, 1971. I had told the story of James's last hours the previous day, as briefly as possible. Readers of biographies don't want long death scenes, like the last acts of operas. I felt I now had to terminate my story swiftly. I wanted some sort of low-keyed peroration. At 10:20 A.M., when the watery winter light was reflected in a hundred glassy windows—the eyes of the towering monsters down the street—I typed a sentence written by James in an essay "Is There a Life After Death?" He believed death was absolute. Like Proust, he had faith in the survival of the consciousness of the artist—in his art. "I reach beyond the laboratory brain," James had written. It seemed a fine statement with which to end. It was, I said, his last word to the untried twentieth century. It was almost as if he had foretold the computer.

The final chord of the quintet's final movement had been struck. I stood up. My back ached. It always does after a long session at the typewriter (two-finger typists do terrible things to their lower back). I stretched. I looked out on the familiar scene, the arrogant architecture; and at the higgledy-piggledy pages I had written, unnumbered, for I'm impatient; I don't like to interrupt myself, even to number a page. Books and papers were piled around me; a chaos of words, out of which I had for so long been creating some kind of order.

I had a sudden feeling of emptiness, as if I had said goodbye to an old friend at an airport and the plane was still on the runway. Then in a swift change of mood, I experienced an inner glow, I suppose the kind of exultation called "a sense of triumph." I had overcome difficulties. I had stuck to my guns. I was free. All the lines could be unplugged from my overworked mental and sensory switchboard.

The dreary day suddenly turned bright, cheerful. I gathered up my sheets and numbered them. I did not reread them. They must be given time to cool off. Then I come to them fresh, usually after twenty-four hours. Sometimes there is a long mopping up. This time I did not anticipate difficulty. Everything seemed in its place; everything seemed right. I could feel it in my bones. The job was done, although a long period would ensue before the book could be in print. I wanted to broadcast to the world this feeling of triumph, especially to those who sadly told me between volumes I had bitten off more than I could chew.

Suddenly I was a man of leisure. I shaved; I picked a bright holiday necktie. Dressed as for festivities I took a long walk—still a great pleasure in New York after all these years. I thought of the books I would write; of promises to publishers. I had a great sense of fulfillment. I went to my club and drank an apéritif. At the bar I greeted a fellow writer with my news. "What will you do now?" he said to me in a voice of catastrophe. He sounded as if my house had burned down, or there had been a death in my family. He talked as if I were unemployed—as if I had lost a life-job. It was the same with others. Most people seemed to think of me as having lost rather than gained my freedom. Few recognized my sense of release.

People used to ask "when will your next volume come out?" The conversation always came to a dead end. "How near are you to ending?" I never knew. They often thought me evasive or secretive. But I really never knew. The book had a life of its own. It had its own periods of gestation. It never revealed its plans to me in advance. What I learned was that art can't be impatient, that craft has its own schedules.

When I say this, I suppose I make some people think I was living inside Henry James's skin all these years. This was never true, save when I was at my writing desk. A biographer, conscious of what he is doing, must be what psychologists call a "participant-observer." He must feel what he is writing, imagine himself to be his characters, and take his perspective.

It is the taking of the perspective that is the true measure of a biography; many of my critics have overlooked this important element in my work. They think I "invested" my being in Henry James; or, as one critic put it, I performed "a rare act of total imaginative bestowal." This was perhaps a soft impeachment, hardly the whole story. The investment was certainly in my subject, but it was even more in the task, not the man. It is all too easy to lose the man in a clutter of documents.

I set out to create a given work, to find an ideal form for my materials, to shape these into a likeness, to reduce them to their essence—and to narrate them fluently. A portrait painter doesn't have to be infatuated with the people whose portraits he paints. The critic who said I had sunk my life into James's had no sense of the enormous appeal of the biographical process itself—it is an infatuation not with subject, but with the story and its telling.

Thinking back on the time-spread of my work, I totaled up my actual writing time. It came to little more than six years. My first volume, *The Untried Years*, was written between 1950–52. The next two volumes, *The Conquest of London* and *The Middle Years*, 1960–61, *The Treacherous Years*, 1967–68, and *The Master*, 1969–71, interrupted by two long visits to Hawaii where I did other writing.

If this was my writing time, what had I done all those other years? Well, a biographer has his own life to lead, as well as the life of his subject. There had been my researches. There had been trips abroad, some for work, some for holiday. There had been various non-Jamesian books to write and edit. And then the wear and tear of daily existence, distractions, illnesses.

There were also longish periods during which I was busy reaping the practical benefits of my reputation, such as it is—barnstorming, visiting colleges, writing reviews, taking care of graduate students, and other professional activities. There is a charming but fanciful legend that I simply lived, breathed, slept, ate Henry James—and did nothing else for twenty years! I find that I saw more than twenty other books through the press during the years I was writing the life of James—not counting prefaces I write to James novels and the twelve-volume collection of his tales I edited.

Looking back, I realize that the biography I have written has had an organic growth. I originally estimated it would take four years. But when I completed *The Untried Years,* George Stevens, Lippincott's editor, was persuasive. I had written, he said, "the young Henry James." Why not publish it at once? It was in reality a fine idea; and I yielded, but not without some nervousness. What if, later on, I wanted to rewrite a chapter? What if a new bundle of letters turned up?

I told myself, however, that if I really had confidence in my estimate of James's character and personality, and if I had captured his childhood, youth and first maturity, my problem would be to show in the sequel his continued growth and development. New material might make for a richer picture, but the "dynamic" of character would remain the same and evolve as James's art evolved. *The Untried Years* was enthusiastically received (though its sale was modest) and justified Stevens's confidence. But it created a great many problems for me.

I had not anticipated, for instance, the deluge of James's letters that flowed into my apartment during 1954 and 1955. Everyone who read my first volume seemed to have a cache of letters in his attic. At one moment I had two thousand holograph letters on my desk, and it took me months to cope with them. I won't speak of the tension induced by the thought of the fire hazard; or the friendly way in which my cat managed always to lie right on top of great batches of them, as if to keep them warm for me. I knew then of seven thousand letters, mainly the Harvard archive. By now I have read fifteen thousand. More turn up constantly.

The new letters forced me to use a "retrospective" method—in a word, a form of the "flashback" adapted to biographical ends. I saw no reason why it would not legitimately serve the ends of biography as it does the writer of fiction. I learned also how to recapitulate, to summarize, to plan transitions from volume to volume, to watch my pace, and use a scenic method.

Instead of freezing myself to a chronology, I sought a kind of Proustian flexibility, moving backward and forward in James's life. The serialization caused me to test all sorts of technical devices, to build thematically and to pay attention to symbolic and mythic detail. The net effect of these experiments with biographical form was that James's life was shown in its evolutionary process. The reader could feel he was growing up with James—and conquering the literary world with him.

My time-spread, the years in which I was busy with other work, allowed a great deal of irrelevance in my material to fall away. This hasn't prevented some from saying I have put "everything" into James's life, and that it is the longest in American literature. The art of biography, at least as I practice it, is an art of leaving out. I have left out enough material to fill many more volumes. We have too many ill-digested lives with long quotations from documents, mainly letters, which when given *in extenso* often contain irrelevant detail and ruin a good "story line." All this required constant thinking through.

When I could work consistently I would go for weeks without writing a line. Then one morning I might suddenly find that a great deal of the clutter had disappeared; a new chapter could be written, telling the essential story. Sometimes trivial facts helped to light up whole areas, serving as "suggestive" detail. The process of selection nevertheless was rigorous. The speed with which I set down my last chapters surprised me; but obviously they had long been written in my inner mind.

"How long, Leon, how long?" asked a friendly English critic at the beginning of his review of my fourth volume. The answer of course, in my case, has been "as long as necessary." By taking my time I benefited in a number of ways. Letters locked away—like Edith Wharton's—were finally unlocked. I was able to write the story of that friendship, so crucial in James's last years, as it had never been told before, out of one hundred and seventy-seven James letters in the Wharton papers at Yale. She herself had ordered them withheld until 1968.

I still receive material that might add little details here and there. But a biographer has to call a halt somewhere or his manuscript would never leave his desk. What this means is that there is plenty left for those who want to do close-ups of certain parts of James's life or deal in detail with friendships which rate only a line or two in the overall economy of my volumes.

The story of my story is a long one, which has involved meeting the members of James's generation who lingered into our own time—Mrs. Wharton, Granville-Barker, Shaw, Yeats and many others, some when I was editing James's plays before I ever planned the biography. And if I were to give a single answer to "what it has meant to write the James quintet" I would say that it has meant the excitement of finding the material, and then the far greater fascination of discovering a form for it: making the reader feel the passage of time; writing a narrative that gives an illusion of a living person and not a figure built out of papier-mâché. I found my personal reward in the imagination of form and structure—so I said in my preface to *The Master*—for, after all, that is the only imagination a biographer can be allowed.

Journeys

Any BIOGRAPHER must of necessity become a pilgrim, a peripatetic, obsessed literary pilgrim, a traveler with four eyes. His essential job is to see through the alien yet friendly vision of his subject, while at the same time constantly seeing for himself. The two ways of looking at the world ultimately become one, the four eyes become two; involved, of course, is the process of matching the inherited verbal record with the actual—in order to create a new verbal record.

For the biographer of Henry James, the pilgrimage is a long and active one. His novels were set in foreign places, in specific villas, in little unnamed towns like the one Lambert Strether visits in *The Ambassadors,* "a thing of whiteness, blueness and crookedness, set in coppery green, and that had the river flowing behind or before it—one could not say which." The author of *English Hours, Italian Hours, A Little Tour in France* and *Portraits of Places* was not only a hardy traveler, he was a sentient one.

Henry James was the archetypal American *flaneur* in Europe, loitering elegantly in many cities visiting country houses, assiduously searching out old ways of life, old manners, old "things." His life, from 1843 to 1916, began in the era of the stagecoach and ended in the age of the motor car; and he had, in that leisurely Victorian world, the patience and personal vision that so many of us have lost. We skim over the world at thirty-five thousand feet and look at beauty through camera lenses. James, the master of mores, always had his Murray or other guide-books in his hand, and he read whatever was related to the *genius loci*. He was never in a hurry. He needed time to drink in "the tone of things."

In his younger years, when Europe seemed far from America and Americans were hungry for stories of travel, he was a genius among travel writers. He supported himself by publishing his travel notes in old American magazines; the generation that grew up on Herman Melville's word-pictures of the Pacific grew old with James's stories of Europe. At various times he found impersonal designations for himself, an affectation not yet out of literary style; he was "the sentimental trav-eler" or, in England, "the observant stranger." In his later years, when he revisited and rewrote, he was, appropriately, the "elderly pilgrim" and "the restless analyst."

It would take a lifetime to follow his foreign foot-steps. That wasn't my purpose. But I did have to be familiar with his *method* of travel, his ways of seeing: I had to make sure of the broad topography of his world. And then I did have to know certain significant houses, villas, *palazzos*. All this led to much carefully budgeted travel in the 1950s and early 1960s, at a time when the student or scholar was much less subsidized than he is today. A career in biography is a costly investment.

I remember reaching a point in writing James's life when I had to visualize the hill of Bellosguardo, over-looking Florence, but could not. I had visited it years before, but now there were matters that had to be made specific in my mind. In particular, the location and relation between two villas referred to by James as the Villa Castellani and the Villa Brichieri.

The Castellani was easy to locate, when I returned to Florence. It stood in a little square at the top of the hill above the Via Romana, and a plaque in the square listed all the celebrities who at one time or another lived nearby—Hawthorne (in the Villa Montauto), James Fenimore Cooper, Henry James and several British and German writers. The Castellanis seem to have come from Spain; by James's time the villa belonged to an old American family. Now it was in other hands and was called the Villa Mercede. The villa figures in *Roderick Hudson,* and more importantly in *The Portrait of a Lady;* the biographical fact I needed was its exact distance from the Villa Brichieri.

I located the Brichieri, still bearing its old name, just below a crest, downhill from the Castellani; it was only about fifty feet away, easily visible from the Castellani garden. The Brichieri is a squarish building, quite isolated, with short scrubby vegetation around it. There is an umbrella pine at one end, as in a landscape by Claude, and beyond, the valley of the Arno.

My purpose in wanting to get the location of these villas in my mind was to try to understand better the friendship between James and the now almost forgotten writer, Constance Fenimore Woolson, a grandniece of Fenimore Cooper. She clearly loved James; he kept a discreet distance from her. But in 1887 he had moved into an apartment in the Brichieri so that he and Miss Woolson, (whom he called familiarly by her literary and ancestral name of Fenimore) were under the same roof. This was no simple "romance," if we may call it that. It was the material that became "The Aspern Papers," the drama of a publisher's pursuit of love letters written by a great poet to his mistress. The publisher attempts to influence the woman through her niece. But James moved the scene of the story to Venice and an old, mouldering *palazzina*. And for his biographer, that meant another search. I knew the villa was in the Rio Marin. I could see it from the railway station, at the end of the Grand Canal. Water bathed its steps, but it was its garden— there was one in front and a small walled one at the back— that determined James's choice of this palace for his setting. There aren't many gardens in Venice. James had been a guest in this little palace; it was the home of an old friend of his Roman days, the American painter and writer, Eugene Benson.

I remember hunting in Venetian churches for certain paintings by Giovanni Bellini, hidden behind altars, that James had ferreted out. They hung exactly where he said they did. I sat in Florian's in the piazza, or in Rome at the Grecco. I visited the Protestant Cemetery in Rome and came first upon graves not in my itinerary, those of Shelley and Keats. My first glimpse of Keats's headstone is unforgettable—"here lies one whose name was writ in water." Nearby I found what I had come for, the simply bordered, violet-covered grave of "Fenimore"; there was the Maltese cross, and nearby, the pyramid of Gaius Cestius, in a place where pagan and Christian mingled. Miss Woolson had committed suicide in Venice and was buried in Rome. In his fiction, James had used the same site to bury his flighty heroine from Schenectady, N.Y., Miss Daisy Miller.

Why does a biographer measure distances between villas, inspect graves and palaces? It is his best way of getting at "the sense of place" he must have. A biographer, unlike a novelist, writes about real places and real people; he may be as imaginative as he pleases, but he must not imagine his facts. And for me to know the two villas between which James and Fenimore moved, and where they lived; to see the facades and gardens and to walk on the terraces and reconstruct the expatriate Florentine life of the late nineteenth century, or the Venetian life of "The Aspern Papers," was to arm myself with such certitudes as are possible to a biographer.

When I came to write I wrote not out of old books but out of visual reality; I had the Arno Valley before my eyes and the vaulted sky, the spacious roccoco rooms, the pebbly terraces—I could almost feel them under foot. I wrote of a small, intricate world with a familiarity I would not otherwise have had—a world in which an emotional drama had taken place whose echoes alone were available to me. I didn't know all the drama. I pieced together the curious relationship out of phrases in letters, scraps of circumstantial evidence, things Fenimore wrote, allusions buried in James's stories. The secrets of Fenimore's life died with her. But James's troubled letters after her death, and his late tale of "The Beast in the Jungle" served to convey states of feeling, and furnish a picture that had ended in the grave in the Protestant cemetery and yielded also "The Altar of the Dead."

There are some aspects of a biographer's subject that would remain hidden even from a thousand eyes. Biographers, contrary to common belief, never know all the answers. They must write their final story out of a network of observation and a patchwork of documents and memories and, in particular, travel into the lost past.

I remember journeying at one time to an English village near Brighton, to be the guest of Dr. Octavia Wilberforce, a friendly descendant of William Wilber-

force, the English antislavery crusader of the early nineteenth century. She was in charge of a rest home for
"tired professional women" founded by her friend, the
American actress and writer Elizabeth Robins, who, in
turn, had known James. The rest home was located in
Miss Robins's Elizabethan farmhouse, and the dairy farm
Dr. Wilberforce ran supported this charitable enterprise.
The doctor herself was a hearty red-cheeked woman, an
early suffragette. She had liberated herself by taking a
medical degree when young women were not welcome
at medical schools.

I found myself cloistered with a group of middle-
aged ex-secretaries and file clerks for a fortnight; it is an
episode I think of as "The Case of the Captive Biographer." The place was called Backsettown, a good name
for a community with a single street and a characteristic
pub.

My interest was focused on a little shack in Dr. Wilberforce's front yard; it was off limits to me. In it were
the books and papers of Elizabeth Robins. Dr. Wilberforce played a cat-and-mouse game with me; there was
no question about who the cat was. She wanted to write
the life of Miss Robins, and she needed my expertise. I
would look at various dull documents every day for her,
give her my opinion, and then she would give me my
reward: she would go to the little shack and return with
a James letter, or a page out of some old notes about
James by Miss Robins.

I had to be very patient, because she also had another,
more profitable market for the documents I sought;
occasionally, they would be auctioned off at Sotheby's to
provide funds for the tired professional women. The result
was I had to seek fragments of this archive elsewhere.

(There was, however, a non-Jamesian dividend: Leonard Woolf lived nearby, and while my interesting conversations with him did little to advance my biographical work, they were a rewarding indulgence for my interest in Virginia Woolf and Bloomsbury.) In the unlikely event that anyone undertakes the literary biography of this biographer of James, my intermittent siege at Backsettown could provide several chapters. It did, in fact, ultimately yield several important sections of my fourth volume of the James life.

My quest for that life also led me to a large French country house near Paris, a splendid house of its type, set in beautiful grounds. It is not the fifty letters I found in the library of the house that I now remember. What I recall is standing at the window of the eighteenth-century drawing room, in this traditional French *maison de campagne,* looking out on the scene while my hostess read to me, in a delightful accent, from one of James's travel essays, a description of a certain country house he had visited, and how he had looked out of the window of the drawing room at the landscape and the dovecote, out of which an occasional dove would circle into the sky. As I looked one of the doves obliged. It was the visual, the concrete, the exquisite, with a Jamesian sound track in a French accent; it also illustrates an ideal situation for the four-eyed traveler, one he does not often find.

I remember going to Chester, near Liverpool, in search of some letters, a splendid batch, in the Public Records Office. The old Roman-medieval town was just as James had described it in his first book, *Transatlantic Sketches* (1875), later redescribed in *The Ambassadors* (1901). Chester was an obligatory stop on the "grand tour" of young

Americans sent abroad by affluent families to receive Continental "polish." They would land at Liverpool and instead of boarding the direct train to London would linger for a day or two at Chester, where the sunshine at best was watery, but where, in addition to Roman ruins, there was a wide wall of the Middle Ages. The place was, so to speak, a blend of Ben Hur and Camelot. I couldn't hear a sermon by the Reverend Charles Kingsley (the author of *Westward Ho!*) as James did, but I visited his fine old church, and stayed at a hotel that seemed very like the one in the opening scene of *The Ambassadors*.

The original is not always at hand. Once I made a trip along the corniche near Genoa to examine an old guest book, but I found only a copy of the book: James's name was in it, but not in his hand—the original doubtless had long before been sold to an autograph dealer.

There are times when a traveling biographer becomes involved in ways beyond the intention of his project. I recall one curious, cold night high over Lerici on the Gulf of Spezia. In the bay below Shelley had drowned. I spent the night there not in quest of Shelley or Byron but of Percy Lubbock, the first editor of the James papers.

I wasn't welcome at the hotel where I stayed; off-season visitors were a nuisance and I suspect that was why they turned on the air-conditioner instead of the heating system. I froze. The next day I found Lubbock in his large villa on the edge of the sea. He was eighty by then and blind. The villa was all open doors and windows—the sea damp was everywhere, and purple islands in the bay seemed wrapped in eternal moisture-weighted air and mist. I looked at mildewed books, and the strange filtered sunshine, and walked on mildewed carpets.

Lubbock now lived out of the world in which his graceful and elegant mind had worked. The author of *The Craft of Fiction* sat in a warm room upstairs, and gave me his reminiscences, tugging at old strings to unwrap parcels of papers. Much of what he told me I already knew from documents I had seen. Yet his blind eyes had looked at certain faces and places and moments in a past I sought.

My trip to see Lubbock remains sharply in my mind—for reasons that have nothing to do with either Lubbock or James. I had driven from Genoa to Spezia through the Bracca Pass—a day's hard drive over vertiginous mountains from which one looked down dizzy cliffs plunging into the sea. I passed peasants carrying huge bundles of firewood, or driving old carts; I circled a small funeral procession, stark, vivid, the old peasant faces, the black clothes, the air of mourning and desolation, the coffin carried slowly to the little church. I drove on roads with hairpin curves and saw in the distance the Carrara mountains white and upright like gigantic teeth biting at the sky. They gave me nightmares that night in Spezia, a vision of natural cruelty and natural beauty.

I doubt whether James ever made this journey; there is irony and perhaps instruction in the fact that as I searched his past—the past he called "visitable"—I underwent an experience entirely for myself that remains the most vivid memory of my travels.

A biographer cannot live inside the skin or vision of his subject and do a decent job of work. No good biographies have ever been written by biographers identified with their subjects. The biographer must remain participant as well as observer, traveling for his own joys.

Yet the four-eyed traveler goes for the duties of his job as well. He must, after all, convert into words the old world of his perception into the new world in which his readers read him. He imbibes atmosphere; he tries to obtain a sense of place and of "pastness." His rewards are often almost meaningless to others. He communicates with the past while everyone else is busy confronting the present. He must read the past but beware of lingering in it. And then he must read past into present—his personal and vicarious travels become a part of a book, an old landscape, a double vision.

Only by keeping his own special vision, his own two eyes, focused and active, can he have the imagination of what has disappeared from this earth. Happily, landscapes and cities do not disappear as rapidly as the men and women who live in them.

The biographer's is really the most intimate kind of travel. It can be a great lark, a series of personal adventures, private, ruminative, felt experience. All belong to the writer's craft and the writer's memory. As with all travel experience it is very hard to make others feel it. Our feelings are our own, as are the inner landscapes where those feelings exist.

No camera can record them; only the language-medium makes possible this kind of travel book—the product of a life lived, and a life relived.

Genesis of a Chapter

AMONG the thousands of letters which Henry James wrote, there is one to an American woman in Paris, who kept a salon in the avenue Gabriel. In this letter I found a few words about certain visitors James entertained in London in the middle 1880s. "There descended upon me from the skies—or rather from Paris," he wrote, "three Frenchmen bearing introductions from Sargent and yearning to see London aestheticism. They were Polignac, Montesquiou and the charming Dr. Pozzi, and to do Sargent's introduction proper honour I put off my departure and devoted Thursday and Friday to entertaining them—which I did I believe successfully." Then toward the end of the letter five more words: "Montesquiou is curious, but slight."

That was all. There was little here to attract a biographer's attention. James was constantly entertaining visitors in London. In the early summer there were the Europe-bound Americans and in the autumn, the same Americans starting for home again. There were also his continental friends who came to London almost as often as he went to Paris. But the name Montesquiou arrested my attention. There was no mistaking the spelling of the name—the *–iou* ending quite different from that other Montesquieu who wrote *L'Esprit des Lois*. This could only have been Count Robert de Montesquiou-Fezensac, who had been a model for Huysmans's character of Des Esseintes in *A Rebours*—that nuanced novel which had such a corrupting influence on Oscar Wilde's *Dorian Gray,* and not a little on Wilde himself. Could this be the same Montesquiou—indeed it had to be—who later became the friend of Proust and was incarnated for posterity in the cultured and charming, the isolent and vicious Baron de Charlus? If so, what was he doing in London?—and in Henry James's company? and why did John Singer Sargent, usually discreet and *comme il faut,* send him to James? And what did James show him of London, "aestheticism"?—with which he was impatient, as he was of anything that dissociated art from life. A search of Montesquiou's verses and memoirs yielded a certain amusement but no light on this matter. It did show an abject admiration for James McNeill Whistler. The Proust-Montesquiou correspondence helped characterize both but offered little help. I had to content myself, with the thought that here was one amusing encounter about which I would never know anything more than that it took place. All I could say was—and was it worth saying?—that during the summer of 1885 James was host in London to three Frenchmen, introduced by Sargent, one of them the flamboyant homosexual aristocrat, Count Robert de Montesquiou.

Still, an encounter between the American and the Frenchman was amusing to contemplate. I searched for the Montesquiou archive in the hope of some James letters but could not track it down. James's remark that Montesquiou was "curious but slight" was of a piece with his other remarks about aesthetes, that word usually implying possible homosexuality. James as we know was a distancing and cautious man; he avoided involvement and was not usually in the habit of cultivating individuals who sought, as Montesquiou did, the perfumes of existence. At the same time he conformed to the rules of politeness and courtesy, and found the hypocrisies and deceits of society both useful and entertaining. He clearly wanted to please Sargent; and he was always eager to be kind to Gallic visitors, given his unbounded interest in the French and their ways.

Disarmed by lack of data, all I could do as a biographer was to speculate about the trio that descended on James in the dense Victorian London of the 1880s. We know it well; it has been chronicled in its sootiness, in the well-dressed top-hatted males and the decorated females; we must put ourselves back into streets crowded with horse-drawn vehicles, a great deal of livery, a great deal of poverty, and the presence of gin mills. Did James and his visitors walk these streets? Did they dine—and if so where? Did James take them to one of his social resources, the music halls? Did he entertain them at his clubs—the Reform or the Athenaeum? No documents, no letters, no records. I could have followed the way of other biographers and set down a long imaginary passage using the word *doubtless,* as some biographers do— doubtless they walked and dined and did this and that: doubtless—the last refuge of biographical ignorance. Such are the exasperations of biography. A single fact teases the mind. But more facts are needed. We learn a little only to discover that we know nothing. The best details seem shut away from us forever.

And yet? Two or three years after pigeonholing Montesquiou and his Proustian companions, I found myself going through batches of letters in Waller Barrett's collection. I came on one letter that was filled with more than the "mere twaddle of graciousness"—which was James's way of describing his socially deceitful letters. In my researches I was often bored by so much epistolary effort: there are moments when one wishes the telephone had been invented earlier—even as today one regrets its invention, since it replaces so many letters we would like to have. The letter I found was addressed to a Miss Boughton, and was written in that vigorous scrawl which denoted haste, a need to be brief—and a failure to achieve this—and a need to be casual. The letter was undated, but I had sufficient clues to know that it was written 3 July 1885.

Dear Miss Boughton:

Excuse a complicated tale—this is my story! Whistler has just this evening been dining with me, in company with two Frenchmen—the Prince de Polignac and the Comte de Montesquiou—to whom he desires greatly to show, on Sunday, the "peacock room" and I have promised him (as he had to go somewhere else) to write to you on the subject so that you should receive the note in the morning. The two Frenchmen aforesaid have been sent to me by a friend in Paris—and I am in a measure responsible for their seeing what they desire, and they desire unspeakably to behold the peacock room. *Therefore,* I hasten on to say that Whistler hoped greatly that you and Mrs. Boughton will lunch with him on *Sunday* at one—or come to him about noon of that day, he then having the Frenchmen with him, to whom he trusts you will make over some pass or permit for Mr. Leyland's house, which you will perhaps have been so good as to obtain in the meanwhile. If Mrs. Boughton and yourself do not come—perhaps you will have been able tomorrow to send the document to him. It seems odd that *I* should be inviting Mrs. Boughton

and you to lunch with Whistler!—especially as I shall not
be there myself, as I return to the country (having been to
London but on a flying visit) tomorrow. But on the whole
nothing that relates to Whistler is queerer than anything
else. Therefore please excuse, and ask Mrs. Boughton, to
whom I send my kind regards to excuse this strange, irregular roundabout communication. The gist of it is that he
(W.) has taken my Frenchmen on his back for a part of
Sunday, that they hunger and thirst to behold the mystic
apartment, that he begs you and Mrs. Boughton to help
him to show it to them (he speaks as if you had all the
facilities for it!) and also, if possible, to lunch with him—
and that I, to further the matter have undertaken to save
time, to write to you! I hope I dont bewilder or bother you
too much, and am ever in haste, very truly yours HENRY
JAMES

Miss Boughton was the daughter of an Anglo-Amer-
ican painter living in London, and the letter to her offered
a new and curious picture: that of Henry James, Whistler and Montesquiou together at a London dinner table.
The juxtaposition of Whistler and Montesquiou further
teased my imagination. Montesquiou had sat for Whistler. I knew the portrait—it is in the Frick Collection.
And I knew that he had been influenced by the American painter. But a Montesquiou eager to see Whistler's
peacocks added to the amusement of my scarce materials. It suggested a peacock in search of a peacock—or,
since we have to accept Whistler's own pictorial emblems,
a peacock in search of a butterfly.

My next bit of research was to find out more about
the peacock room. I knew that Whistler had painted the
ornate birds in Leyland's house. I was not at first aware
that these had been preserved—but I soon discovered

that the entire Peacock Room, thanks to the energies of Charles L. Freer, the founder of the Freer Gallery of Art (now a part of the Smithsonian Institution) had been established permanently in the gallery in Washington. So off I went to see what Montesquiou had so ardently sought. The story of this part of Whistler's creation is to be found in all the biographies of the American master, and most versions agree on the essentials. The peacock room was painted for the shipping tycoon Leyland, a renowned patron of the arts. He had built a large house at 49 Prince's Gate in London, and employed several artists of the late Victorian period to decorate it. Whistler had painted panels along the staircase. And his canvas, *La Princesse du Pays de la Porcelaine,* painted in 1863–64, was purchased by Leyland to be placed in the dining room, opposite some magnificent blue and white porcelain of which Leyland was an enthusiastic collector. *La Princesse* belonged to the earlier Whistler period when he was frequenting Rossetti and the pre-Raphaelites: but it is markedly influenced by Japanese art which, as we know, Whistler had studied with close attention.

The painting shows the standing figure of a woman in a kimono; behind her is a screen that constitutes the middle background of the panel. The kimono is rose-orange and it hangs loosely off the arms of the woman who wears a robe of silver-gray and pink, held by a red sash. She stands on a blue-cream rug which harmonizes with her dress. The woman's hair is black, the head resembling the women of Rossetti; the fan is a cream white against the background screen which is painted in a lower value of cream white with flower decorations, and in the background one sees one half of a blue jar. The picture is signed simply "Whistler 1864"—the but-

terfly signature had not yet begun to flutter in the corner
of his canvases.

This was the painting which Leyland proposed to
hang in his dining room. Whistler could not complain.
He was well represented in this magnificent house. But
the decoration of the room was entrusted to a less soaring and less egotistical imagination, a decorator and
architect named Jeckyll.

Jeckyll had procured for a thousand pounds some
historic leather brought to England by Catherine of
Aragon, displaying her device of small, richly colored
red flowers and pomegranates. Whistler gazed uneasily
at the room. To have his rose and silver placed opposite
the blue and white porcelain was one thing. To have this
orientally delicate yet robust work surrounded by Spanish leather and red flowers would be a chronic irritation.
The flowers, he told Leyland, killed the pale tones of his
Princesse. Leyland gave him permission to repaint the
flowers and Whistler promptly changed the red to gold.
The result was horrible. Jeckyll complained. Whistler
admitted it was a mistake. The Leylands were leaving
for the summer and Whistler was left in charge of the
work. He promised to rectify the inharmonious effect of
the gold flowers, Spanish leather and the Japanese-inspired
painting of his princess in the land of porcelain. He lost
no time. He brought his assistants to the house, erected
scaffolding and went to work. He found the Spanish
leather an enchanting surface. What took shape on it
were several large peacocks painted in blue and gold.
And so he named his work in his characteristic way—
Harmony in Blue and Gold.

Leyland was not altogether unaware that certain gross

changes were taking place by the time he returned. The conversion of the dining room was the talk of London. Strangers had begun ringing the bell asking to see it. Whistler had been welcoming them as if he were running an art show. Royalty turned up as well. Leyland seems to have held aloof, but he was reported hurt by some depreciatory language Whistler used suggesting he was a *parvenu*. The shipping magnate's revenge was subtle. When Whistler asked for two thousand guineas for his work, Leyland said it was too much. They would not have argued over the thousand he finally paid if he had paid in guineas, as professionals are paid in Britain. He paid in pounds. Whistler was being treated as if he were a tradesman. He pocketed the money and promptly retaliated. His finishing touch to the dining room was to paint a heap of gold coins under the claw of the peacock. Leyland would face the monetary bird as he dined. It is to Leyland's credit that he did not have this painted over.

An entertaining story, but not altogether relevant in all its detail to the life of James; simply a gloss to his amusing letter to Miss Boughton. I had thus a great deal of background for my anecdote; indeed more background than foreground. Only one other document turned up. There came a moment when I was examining a handful of letters written *to* James. A few—perhaps two hundred—of the letters written to him survived the bonfire of his papers. Among these I found the letter from Sargent introducing Montesquiou. It was of 29 June 1885 and dated from Paris.

I remember that you once said that an occasional Frenchman was not an unpleasant diversion to you in London, and I have been so bold as to give a card of introduction to you to two friends of mine. One is Dr. S. Pozzi the man in the red gown (not always) a very brilliant creature, and the other is the unique extrahuman Montesquiou of whom you may have heard Bourget speak with bitterness, but who was to Bourget to a certain extent what Whistler is to Oscar Wyld. (Take warning and do not bring them together.) They are going to spend a week in London and I fancy Montesquiou will be anxious to see as much of Rossetti's and Burne Jones' work as he can. I have given him a card to B.J. and to the Comyns Carrs and to Tadema.

The Sargent letter had an interest (and not least his spelling of Oscar Wilde's name). I went back to the Frick Collection to see Whistler's portrait of Montesquiou painted several years after the meeting in London. The canvas is awkwardly hung, very high, so that one gets a sense of an elongated elegant and arrogant figure, holding a coat over his arm, and one sees the glossy surface, a gaunt debonair individual, a walking stick. Nevertheless it gave me an impression of the butterfly's vision of the peacock.

These were my documents and my large background. I had investigated Polignac and found little in his career relevant to my story. Pozzi I found was amiable and hearty, and James liked him. At a later date they met in Paris. And then the three were to cross in the future the path of Marcel Proust, who at the time of which I was writing was a boy of fourteen. He had probably met James in the home of Alphonse Daudet.

There came a moment when I had to make up my mind. I was trying to tell the story of the American novelist in London in the mid-eighties, and to suggest the peopled life he led, after taking root in England, and to capture the flavor of that time. I wanted to characterize his easy cosmopolitanism, his links with the French, his friendship with Sargent, his casual encounters with Whistler. In his early London days he liked breakfasting on Sundays at Whistler's in Chelsea because the artist served pancakes and tomatoes. And in these materials I began to see a brief episodic chapter, a "fun-chapter" one might say, tame enough to be sure, but having some possibility of being pictorial and illustrative. That amusing letter which unlocked the peacock room for me, and Sargent's little note, gave some indication of James's relationship to the artists, and then there was the comedy of Montesquiou and Whistler, an encounter that had ironic and comic elements even if I had none of the details—with James in the role of introducer and factotum. There was a neat fund of the light and comic in all this, and a biographer cannot overlook an opportunity for a touch of comedy. I would have given much for a few words and phrases of the talk between Whistler, Montesquiou and their American host around the table of the Reform Club—but that was irretrievable, as all dinner table conversations are.

All I could do was evoke the persons involved and leave it to the reader to imagine the monocled Whistler, the painted and mustachioed French dandy, and the grave and bulky James. My finding much later, in a new biography of Montesquiou, of two James letters written to the Count added little. Montesquiou seems to have written James an effusive thank-you note and James replied with a flourish that England might seem to have a dull surface, but this was a mask—*un masque trompeur des jouissances qui vous attendent.* What seemed most ironic of all was that the American novelist in the eighties spent his two days with three of Proust's future characters. It was a case of a novelist of the nineteenth century consorting with the real life personages of a future fiction. That seemed justification enough for my chapter.

Notes

IN *Writing Lives* I have brought together all my writings on biography which I wish to preserve. The book in a sense is a counterpart to my gathering-in of my papers in literary psychology, *Stuff of Sleep and Dreams* (1981), which dealt in a large measure with biographical psychology. Into this volume I have incorporated, in a much revised and rearranged way, my five lectures published long ago as *Literary Biography*. That book of 1957 was expanded and reprinted in 1959. It contained my Alexander Lectures on the writing of lives dealing with individuals who were themselves writers. It was, I later learned, a unique study: that aspect of biography had never been isolated from general biography, and it was reprinted in 1973. In reprinting it once again, I have added five other papers dealing with Subject, Transference, Archives, Myth and Narratives. I have also in certain portions of the *Literary Biography* sections made revisions that are tantamount to making them new. My object has been to define more widely than I did earlier the nature of what we can call the New Biography.

The notes which follow are general and not detailed. For a long time I kept a commonplace book in which I wrote quotations from various sources dealing with biography. Since I kept this book for myself, I never took the trouble to put down the exact work from which I was quoting, although I always made the necessary attribution to the authors. In some instances I am now at a loss to say where I found this quote from Byron or that from George Eliot. But where sourcing is possible I have performed it in the traditional way.

The epigraph from Virginia Woolf on writing lives is from a letter written by her to her sister Vanessa, *Letters* Vol. 6, 245.

INTRODUCTION

My Introduction in the Form of a Manifesto is a much revised version of a manifesto published in Vol. 1 No. 1 of the journal *Biography,* an interdisciplinary quarterly, Honolulu, Winter, 1978.

"Ordinary lives"—in a sense anyone's life can be made the subject of a biography. Certain social scientists and psychologists have urged the writing of lives of the "obscure"—individuals whose private heroisms belong simply to their existence. I tend to regard these as assuming in most instances the nature of "case histories." The nature of a biography is most often predetermined by the existence of documents and archives.

THE NEW BIOGRAPHY

This section first appeared as "Principia Biographica, Notes for a Preface" in a festschrift for the biographer Edgar Johnson, *From Smollett to James* (1981). I expanded it into a keynote address titled "Biography and the Science of Man" for an international symposium on biography held in Honolulu in January 1981. It was later published in *New Directions in Biography* (ed. Friedson 1981).

Virginia Woolf on her writing *Roger Fry, Letters* Vol. 6, 374.

Strachey: see his introduction to *Eminent Victorians* (1918).

The quotations here used by Yeats, Eliot (George and T.S.), Nabokov and others on biography are unsourced in my commonplace book.

Henry James, Shakespeare's curse: see Appendix 4 to Henry James *Letters* Vol. IV, (1984).

Thackeray—Gordon N. Ray I *The Uses of Adversity* (1955), II *The Age of Wisdom* (1958).

Percy Lubbock, *The Craft of Fiction* (1921).

Michelet wrote that he wished to make the silences of history speak. His exact words were *Je veux faire parler les silences de l'histoire.*

Virginia Woolf's essays on biography were published in her posthumous volume *Granite and Rainbow* (1958).

Sigmund Freud "a new province"—see the chapter on Biography and Psychoanalysis. The other principles enunciated here are dealt with in the chapters on Transference, Myth and Narrative.

DILEMMAS

This chapter is derived from the first chapter in *Literary Biography* (1959).

Lytton Strachey's *Eminent Victorians* contains an admirable and much-quoted preface which may be read as an early manifesto for the New Biography.

The following studies in recent years throw light and help to define modern biography: Richard D. Altick, *Lives and Letters* (1965); Catherine Drinker Bowen, *Biography, The Craft and the Calling* (1969); James L. Clifford, *From Puzzles to Portraits* (1970); James L. Clifford (ed.), *Biography as an Art* (1962);

Helen Gardner, "Literary Biography," *In Defence of the Imagination* (1982); John A. Garraty, *The Nature of Biography* (1957); Robert Gittings, *The Nature of Biography* (1978); Paul Murray Kendall, *The Art of Biography* (1965); André Maurois, *Apsects of Biography* (1929); Harold Nicolson, *The Development of English Biography* (1927); Dennis W. Petrie, *Ultimately Fiction,* (1981); Donald J. Winslow, *Life-Writing: A Glossary of Terms* (1980).

BOSWELL

A portion of the first section of *Literary Biography* is incorporated in this chapter. I have brought together from other sections various mentions of Boswell. The chapter also includes a portion of a review I wrote in 1966 of Frederick A. Pottle's *James Boswell: The Earlier Years* (1966) which appeared in *Saturday Review,* 30 April 1966, 30–31.

James and Lowell: see *Essays in London* (1893) which included Henry James's memorial essay.

My quotations from Boswell's *Life of Samuel Johnson L.L.D.* are from the Oxford Edition (1904).

For the Young episode see Boswell II 420–422; also 118–119. For the discussion of literary lives see Boswell II 405; for the 1776 journey see Boswell II 3–4.

SUBJECT

This section represents a recasting of the "Subject" chapter in *Literary Biography*. It appeared in the 1981 special issue on biography of the English journal *Prose Studies* together with my summaries of the transference problem in Lytton Strachey and Van Wyck Brooks. The article was entitled "Biographer and Subject: Lytton Strachey and Van Wyck Brooks," 281–293.

The transference problem: Sigmund Freud, *Leonardo da Vinci* (1910); I am quoting from the Brill translation of 1947, 111–12.

Johnson's *Lives of the Poets.* See Boswell II 105.

TRANSFERENCE

Transference defined: see James Drever, *A Dictionary of Psychology* (1952).

André Maurois' lectures on biography were delivered during May 1928 in Trinity College, Cambridge. The passages quoted here are from the texts of these lectures, especially the chapter titled "Biography as a Means of Expression." See *Aspects of Biography* (1929) 115–144.

Mark Schorer wrote *Sinclair Lewis: An American Life* (1961) and his essay on his transference problem, entitled "The Burdens of Biography," appears in *The World We Imagine* (1969) 221–239.

Lawrance Thompson, *Selected Letters of Robert Frost* (1964) 530.

The sections of this chapter on Lytton Strachey and Van Wyck Brooks first appeared in *Prose Studies,* Leicester, England, (1983). The biographical details here given are derived from Michael Holroyd, *Lytton Strachey* (2 vols. 1967); Charles Richard Sanders, *Lytton Strachey* (1957) and from my *Bloomsbury, A House of Lions* (1979). The section on Brooks is derived from my personal talks and memories of Brooks and from James Hoopes's *Van Wyck Brooks* (1977). See also Brooks's three volume autobiography, *Scenes and Portraits* (1954), *Days of the Phoenix* (1957) and *From the Shadow of the Mountain* (1961). Edmund Wilson's comments on Brooks and Henry James are to be found in *The Shores of Light* (1952) 217–228.

ARCHIVES

The original version of this chapter was delivered as one of the "Monday Evening Papers" at the Center for Advanced Studies, Wesleyan University, No. 7 in the series, 11 October 1965, Paul Horgan presiding. It has been considerably revised for inclusion here. The passage on presidential libraries was not included in the original paper.

Richard Ellmann: in his address, 1960, receiving the National Book Award for his life of Joyce.

See Richard D. Altick *Lives and Letters* for the passage on Damon's life of Amy Lowell, 371–372.

Strachey's little bucket. See the preface to *Eminent Victorians*.

QUEST

This chapter is reprinted from *Literary Biography*.

A.J.A. Symons, *The Quest for Corvo* (1934) 27–29.

Arthur and Barbara Gelb, *O'Neill* (1962).

Norman Holmes Pearson, "Problems of Literary Executorship," in *Studies in Bibliography,* Papers of the Bibliographical Society, University of Virginia, V (1952–53). Hervey Allen's letter is on page 10.

For a full discussion of James's epistolary strategies see Leon Edel, Henry James *Letters* I (1974) xiii–xxxvi. Also *Selected Letters of Henry James* (ed. Edel, 1955) xv–xxxi.

The account of Henry James's burning of his papers is given in *The Master,* Vol. V of *The Life of Henry James* (1972), 437. For Dicken's destruction of his papers see Edgar Johnson, *Charles Dickens, His Tragedy and Triumph,* II (1952) 963.

James's essay on George Sand, the first of three dealing with the novelist, appeared in *Notes on Novelists* (1914) 168–169.

Sir James Mackenzie, *Angina Pectoris* (1923) 209–210: "Case 97. Male. Aged 66. Examined 25 February 1909." The unpublished letter from Mackenzie to Dr. Harold Rypins is dated 12 January 1925 and was written a week before the physician's death. See also R. MacNair Wilson, *The Beloved Physician, Sir James Mackenzie* (1926). A posthumous paper on Mackenzie and James by Dr. Rypins was edited by me and appeared in *American Literature* entitled "Henry James in Harley Street," XXIV, No. 4 (January 1953) 481–492.

"Nothing would induce me." James, *Notes of a Son and Brother,* (1914) X.

"Blood and thunder tale." G.W. James to his parents in *Alice James: Her Brothers, Her Journal* (1934) 36.

Percy Lubbock (ed.) *The Letters of Henry James* (1920). In his introduction Lubbock quotes a memorandum from T.S. Perry: "He was continually writing stories, mainly of a romantic kind. The heroes were for the most part villains, but they were white lambs by the side of the sophisticated heroines, who seemed to have read all Balzac in the cradle and to be positively dripping with lurid crimes."

"Avowed authorship." Virginia Harlow, *Thomas Sergeant Perry* (1950) 272–273.

Mrs. John Hall Wheelock of New York generously read through her grandmother's letters to her father, the writer and critic, Charles De Kay. The passage in the letter of 29 February 1864 reads: "Miss Elly Temple has just come in looking very fresh and pretty—Henry James has published a story in the February Continental, called a Tragedy of Errors. read it. Smith v[an] Buren forbade Ellie to read it! which brought a smile of quiet contempt to Harry's lips but anger and indignation to those of Miss Minnie Temple." Elly and Minnie Temple were Henry James's cousins. Smith Van Buren, a son of U.S. President Martin Van Buren, had married into the James family and was therefore an uncle of the Temple girls and of Henry James.

"A Tragedy of Error" appears unsigned in the *Continental*

Monthly, a journal "devoted to literature and national policy," V (Feb. 1864), no. 2, 204–16. The editor of the journal at the time the story appeared was Mrs. Martha Elizabeth Duncan Walker Cook. One of the main purposes of the magazine was "to advocate emancipation as a political necessity." For my discussion of the story see *Henry James: The Untried Years* (1953), the chapter titled "Ashburton Place." The story was reprinted in the *New England Quarterly,* XXIX, no. 3 (Sept. 1956) with a prefatory note by me.

CRITICISM

This chapter has been abridged from *Literary Biography.*

Virginia Woolf, *Orlando* (1928) 189–190.

Henry James in his review of Ernest Daudet's *Mon Frere et moi,* in *Atlantic Monthly* XLIX (June 1882) 846–851.

W.B. Yeats *Autobiographies* (1955).

Orlando 17–18.

Douglas Bush, "John Milton," *English Institute Essays* 1946 5–19.

T.S. Eliot, "The Function of Criticism," in *Selected Essays* (1932).

C.A. Sainte-Beuve, *Nouveaux Lundis,* III (Paris 1865): "La littérature, la production littéraire, n'est point pour moi distincte ou du moins séparable du reste de l'homme et de l'organisation; je puis goûter une oeuvre, mais il m'est difficile de la juger indépendamment de la connaissance de l'homme même; et je dirais volontiers tel arbre, tel fruit. L'étude littéraire me mène ainsi tout naturellement à l'étude morale."

PSYCHOANALYSIS

I have retained very little of my chapter in *Literary Biography* dealing with psychoanalysis. The present chapter, which substitutes for it, comprises later writings on this subject, notably "The Nature of Literary Psychology" published in the *Journal of the American Psychoanalytic Association* (Vol. 29, No. 2, 447–67) and "Toward a Theory of Literary Psychology" in *Interpersonal Explorations in Psychoanalysis* (ed. Witenberg 1973) 343–54. See also my essay on biography and psychoanalysis in *Biography as an Art*. (ed. Clifford 1962) 226–239.

Sigmund Freud, *Letters* (ed. Ernst L. Freud 1960) 391.

Coleridge: see I.A. Richards *Coleridge on Imagination* (1935); Kathleen Coburn's Alexander Lectures, *Experience into Thought: Perspectives in the Coleridge Notebooks* (1979).

Henry James: the "deep well of unconscious cerebration." See his preface to *The American* in *The New York Edition* of his novels and tales II vii reprinted in *The Art of the Novel* (ed. Blackmur 1932) 23. "I was charmed with my idea, which would take, however, much working out; and precisely because it had so much to give, I think I must have dropped it for the time into the deep well of unconscious cerebration." The novelist adds that he hoped the idea would emerge "from that reservoir" i.e. the unconscious "with a firm iridescent surface and a notable increase of weight." This is an admirable and precise account of the artist's sense of his unconscious as the "reservoir" of his creations. See also James's letter to Dr. James J. Putnam in *Letters* IV (1984) 594–598.

Edmund Wilson. See *The Twenties* (ed. Edel 1975) for an account of Wilson's nervous breakdown and subsequent sojourn at Clifton Springs sanatorium in New York 491–495.

Freud and Lytton Strachey. See Michael Holroyd *Strachey* II 615–616. Also Edel, *Bloomsbury, a House of Lions* 228.

Dr. Alfred Adler. Edel, *Stuff of Sleep and Dreams* (1982) 7–11.

Dr. Phyllis Greenacre, *The Quest for the Father* (1963) 10–12.

Ernest Jones, *The Life and Work of Sigmund Freud*. See Edel, "The Biographer and Psychoanalysis," *International Journal of Psychanalysis,* 13 (1961) Nos. 4–5, 458–466.

George Moraitis M.D., "A Psychoanalyst's Journey into a

Historian's World; an Experiment in Collaboration," Chicago: *The Annual of Psychoanalysis* VII (1979) 287–320.

MYTH

The first portion of this chapter is derived from a paper "The Figure Under the Carpet" which I delivered at a symposium on biography at the National Portrait Gallery, Smithsonian Institution in 1978, later published in *Telling Lives (ed. Pachter 1979) 16–34*. The sections on Thoreau and Rex Stout derive from papers published in *Stuff of Sleep and Dreams* (1982). 25–28 and "The Mystery of Walden Pond" 47–65.

For the portion on Balzac and his myth I used a part of my review of Maurois' *Prometheus, The Life of Balzac,* published originally in the *Bulletin of the Hudson Book Club* (No. 162, 1966).

My discussion of Ralph Ellison, Martin Luther King and Mackenzie King is derived from some notes I made when I was reading C.P. Stacey, *A Very Double Life, The Private World of Mackenzie King* (1976).

NARRATIVES

Form: This section appeared in *Literary Biography* in the chapter called "Time."

Geoffrey Scott, *The Portrait of Zélide* (1925).

Percy Lubbock, *Portrait of Edith Wharton* (1947).

Fiction: This section derives from the second part of "Time" in *Literary Biography.* Hugh Kenner, review of *Parts of a World: Wallace Stevens Remembered* (Brazeau 1983) in Washington Post *Book World,* 27 November 1983.

Virginia Woolf, *Orlando* (1928) 62, 91–93, 123, 174–75, 189–190, 277.

Virginia Woolf, *Diary* III 1925–1930 (1980) 168, 176–177, 203; *Diary* IV 1931–1935 (1982) 40, 144.

See also Victoria Glendinning, *Vita: The life of Vita Sackville-West,* (1983); Knole: see Aileen Pippett, *The Moth and the Star* (1940) Chapter XIV; Frank Baldanza, "Orlando and the Sackvilles," *PMLA,* LXX No. 1 (March 1955) 274279; and V. Sackville-West, *Knole and the Sackvilles* (1922).

Rupert Hart-Davis, *Hugh Walpole: A Biography* (1952).

Henry James to Grace Norton. *Letters* I (ed. Edel, 1974) 245: Ralph L. Rusk, *The Life of Ralph Waldo Emerson* (1949); Henry James, *Italian Hours* (1909) 293; James, "The Correspondence of Carlyle and Emerson," *Century Magazine XXVI (July 1883) 384–395 also review of J.E. Cabot's Memoir of Ralph Waldo Emerson* (1887) in *Macmillan's Magazine* (LVII (December 1887) 86–98, reprinted under the title of "Emerson" in *Partial Portraits (1888).*

Maurois, Aspects, Tolstoi and Napoleon, 190–193.

Fact: This section derives from my essay "Biography: The Question of Form" published in *Friendship's Garland* (Rome 1966), essays in honor of Mario Praz, 343–360.

Virginia Woolf on her writing of the biography of Roger Fry, in *A Writer's Diary* (1953) 79, 113–114, 116–117.

THE PERSONAL WORKSHOP

"Writing the Quintet" appeared in the *New York Times Book Review* under the title "The Final Chord of the Quintet" 6 February 1972. It has been revised.

"Journeys" appeared in the *Times* travel section 21 January 1973 under the title "A Biographer's Trip to the Past is *Déjà Vu* with a Difference." It has been revised.

"Genesis of a Chapter" is a hitherto unpublished paper. The chapter referred to appeared in the third volume of my *Life of Henry James* where it bears the title "The Peacock and the Butterfly." (*The Middle Years,* 1962)

Index

INDEX

INDEX